that's what she said

* * *

The Most Versatile Joke on Earth

Justin Wishne
and Bryan Nicolas

Creators of TWSSstories.com

A PLUME BOOK

PLUME
Published by the Penguin Group
Penguin Group (USA) Inc., 375 Hudson Street, New York, New York 10014, U.S.A.
• Penguin Group (Canada), 90 Eglinton Avenue East, Suite 700, Toronto, Ontario,
Canada M4P 2Y3 (a division of Pearson Penguin Canada Inc.) • Penguin Books Ltd.,
80 Strand, London WC2R 0RL, England • Penguin Ireland, 25 St. Stephen's Green,
Dublin 2, Ireland (a division of Penguin Books Ltd.) • Penguin Group (Australia),
250 Camberwell Road, Camberwell, Victoria 3124, Australia (a division of Pearson
Australia Group Pty. Ltd.) • Penguin Books India Pvt. Ltd., 11 Community Centre,
Panchsheel Park, New Delhi – 110 017, India • Penguin Group (NZ), 67 Apollo Drive,
Rosedale, North Shore 0632, New Zealand (a division of Pearson New Zealand
Ltd.) • Penguin Books (South Africa) (Pty.) Ltd., 24 Sturdee Avenue, Rosebank,
Johannesburg 2196, South Africa

Penguin Books Ltd., Registered Offices: 80 Strand, London WC2R 0RL, England

First published by Plume, a member of Penguin Group (USA) Inc.

First Printing, June 2011
10 9 8 7 6 5 4 3 2 1

 REGISTERED TRADEMARK—MARCA REGISTRADA

LIBRARY OF CONGRESS CATALOGING-IN-PUBLICATION DATA

Wishne, Justin.
    That's what she said : the most versatile joke on earth / Justin Wishne and Bryan
Nicolas.
        p. cm.
    ISBN 978-0-452-29714-2 (pbk. : alk. paper) 1. "That's what she said" jokes.
I. Nicolas, Bryan. II. Title.
    PN6231.T567W58 2011
    818'.60208—dc22   2010046918

Printed in the United States of America

BOOKS ARE AVAILABLE AT QUANTITY DISCOUNTS WHEN USED TO PROMOTE PRODUCTS OR SERVICES.
FOR INFORMATION PLEASE WRITE TO PREMIUM MARKETING DIVISION, PENGUIN GROUP (USA) INC., 375
HUDSON STREET, NEW YORK, NEW YORK 10014.

A PLUME BOOK

THAT'S WHAT SHE SAID

In May 2009, JUSTIN WISHNE and BRYAN NICOLAS founded the website TWSSstories.com to provide people all over the world with a way to share the "that's what she said" jokes that come up in everyday conversations. Justin and Bryan are both graduates of the University of Illinois at Urbana-Champaign and currently reside and work in Chicago.

Contents

Foreword   vii

Acknowledgments   ix

Introduction: When Did She Start Talking?   xi

At School
   She's Got Class   1

At Work
   Don't Worry, She's a Professional   25

Gets Wet
   Bodies of Water and Wet Bodies   43

Goes Wild
   She's a Dirty Girl   57

Hits the Road
   She Really Gets Around   67

Falling in Love
   It's Not You, It's Her   79

Contents

Goes Out to Eat
Eating Out with Her   93

Fun and Games
She's Very Active . . . In More Ways Than One   113

That's What *He* Said
Sometimes He's Doing All the Talking   129

In Popular Culture
She's So Hot Right Now   145

Throughout History
Famous Quotes from Dirty Minds   155

Appendix 1: Add Your Own!   161

Appendix 2: The That's What She Said Personality Quiz   171

Foreword

Over the years, a lot of things have come out of my mouth, but it was only recently that I started to gain notoriety for my many oral indiscretions. Now, when people ask me about my rise to fame, I tell them that it started out small, and then before long it became bigger than I ever could have imagined, until finally it downright exploded. Usually these sorts of things happen gradually, with a slow and steady buildup, but in my case it all happened way too fast—I only wish I had a chance to brace myself for what was to come.

One day I was minding my own business, and the next thing you know, I couldn't walk down the street without someone screaming my name and begging me to come and talk to them. I must admit that it was a strange sensation to get used to at first, but after I got over the initial discomfort and awkwardness of these encounters, I quickly found myself enjoying every minute of it.

Foreword

It always gives me great pleasure to recount the many people I've been able to satisfy with my unique oral abilities, so when the authors of *That's What She Said* asked me to give them a hand, I immediately jumped at the chance. The process of picking out the best quotes that have been attributed to me over the years was a long and hard one—I had to struggle to make sure I got it all down—but when I look back at the end result, I can't help but smile. Take it from me: When you've seen as many as I have, it takes a lot to impress you . . . and this collection comes out on top.

 *She*

Acknowledgments

The authors would like to thank their families and friends for their support over the years as well as during the process of writing this book. In addition, special thanks goes out to Lisa Joley for believing in us and helping to make this project a reality. We'd also like to thank Chad Brown, without whom TWSSstories.com never would have gotten off the ground.

Thanks to our agent, Holly Schmidt, and our editor, Nadia Kashper, along with her team at Plume, for all of their hard work and dedication in getting this book to print.

To all of the "that's what she said" fans around the world who have submitted their TWSS Stories, we thank you for your continued patronage—we could never have gotten this far without your support.

Finally, we'd like to thank the talented writers and cast of *The Office* for providing the inspiration behind TWSSstories.com and this book.

Introduction: When Did She Start Talking?

What most people don't know is that she hasn't closed her mouth in over a hundred years. She started as a theater actress in Britain, circa 1900, struggling to make a living and doing whatever, and whomever, it took to make it big. Feeling sinful, she began confessing her many sexual escapades to the clergy. Soon, word of her exploits spread, and across the land people coined a phrase to refer to her promiscuous tendencies: "as the actress said to the bishop." The phrase first appeared in print in 1928, as the catchphrase of Simon Templar (aka The Saint) in *Meet the Tiger*, the inaugural book in a series of crime novels by Leslie Charteris.

One year later, in 1929, Alfred Hitchcock used another variant of the joke in a screen test for the film *Blackmail*. In the film clip, Hitchcock is seen flirting with leading lady Anny Ondra, when he says, "Come here, stand in your place, otherwise it will not come out right . . . as the girl said to the soldier."

Over the next several decades, "as the actress said to the bishop" maintained a small underground following in the UK but almost slipped into obscurity.

Though there is no consensus on the origin of the Americanized version, "that's what she said," the phrase hit the big time in the early 1990s in *Wayne's World*:

Garth Algar: (*holding a picture of Claudia Schiffer*) Hey, are you through yet, because I'm getting tired of holding this.

Wayne Campbell: Yeah, that's what she said.

The film gave a whole new audience the perfect, easy way to inject sexual innuendo into otherwise innocent, everyday conversations. But, unfortunately, popularity is a fickle mistress, and despite its brief emergence into the limelight, the phrase failed to endure. In the years that followed, "that's what she said" made guest appearances on shows like *Family Guy* and *King of the Hill*, but it just didn't stick.

Around the same time, "as the actress said to the bishop" was experiencing a resurgence in the UK thanks to the sense of humor of a man by the name of David Brent (portrayed by Ricky Gervais), a regional manager at Wernham Hogg, on the original, UK version of *The Office*. A few years later, as an homage to his British counterpart,

Michael Scott (played by Steve Carell) brought the American equivalent of the joke across the pond to Scranton, Pennsylvania, and the employees of Dunder Mifflin.

"That's what she said" made its debut on *The Office* on September 27, 2005, in an episode called "Sexual Harassment." The joke is repeated three times throughout the episode, the most memorable of which is the exchange that takes place as Michael Scott is announcing his "retirement from comedy," at corporate's urging:

Michael Scott: When we talk about things here, we must only discuss work-associated things. And you can consider this my retirement from comedy. In the future, if I want to say something funny, or witty, or make an impression, I will no longer, *ever*, do any of those things.

Jim Halpert: Does that include "that's what she said"?

Michael: Um, hmm. Yes.

Jim: Wow, that is really hard. You really think you can go all day long? Well, you always left me satisfied and smiling, so . . .

Michael: That's what she said!

The joke would appear on the show dozens of times in the seasons that followed.

Introduction

In this book, we've gathered together some of the funniest and most original "that's what she said" jokes sent to TWSSstories.com. The situations are real, the conversations are true, and we hope you enjoy this tribute to what is destined to become the most timeless joke of all time.

that's what
she said

* * *

At School

She's Got Class

I was taking an essay test when a girl raised her hand and half-jokingly said, "Can we finish this orally? My hand is starting to hurt." TWSS

In English class, a girl volunteered to read her story out loud. She started, "It was hard. And something I'd never done before." TWSS

I was in biology class and we had to make pie charts of our data, including a sliver of a section that was 0.25 percent. One girl got really frustrated and said, "It's sooo hard! I can't fit it in, it's just too small." Our bio teacher, seeing that she was in distress, said, "Wait, I'm coming!" TWSS

My friend and I were in home ec learning how to sew. My friend was having a hard time getting the string through the needle, so she asked the teacher for help. The teacher gave my friend her own needle to try instead. My friend got the string in with no problem and the teacher said, "Oh, I guess my hole was just big enough for you to fit it in." TWSS

Today my P.E. teacher combined classes with the yoga teacher. The yoga teacher was doing this weird stretch, and I said, "That position looks awkward." She replied, "Oh, it looks super awkward for people watching, but it feels great when you're doing it." TWSS

My friends and I were doing math homework and checking our answers from the previous day's assignment. I asked my friend about #70 and her response was, "Well, I got to 69 and I got confused, so I stopped." TWSS

For my chemistry exam we had to explain the principle workings of a straw. After the test, I told my friend about the question. She replied, "That's easy! You suck on it, the stuff comes into your mouth, and then you swallow." TWSS

I was in social studies class today and we had to do a presentation about some current events articles. One boy did his about a man who got arrested for trying to shove a brick down a woman's throat. My friend yelled out to the class, "Why would anyone want to shove something that big in someone's mouth?" TWSS

We were about to take a quiz and my psych teacher says, "You have fifteen minutes to do it. It probably won't take you that long, though." TWSS

Today in physics class, my friend Ryan was playing with a spring from a pen. He squeezed it and said, "If I do this any longer it's gonna shoot in someone's face." TWSS

In my Spanish class we all got Jolly Ranchers. Someone asked why his was all sticky and another guy said, "Suck on it a little longer and it will become hard." TWSS

In Spanish class we were filling out a crossword puzzle and one of the words didn't fit. I asked my friend and she said, "It didn't fit in mine either, but I just stuck it in." TWSS

I was in math class and we were starting a new unit when my ex-girlfriend said, "This is soo hard." My teacher replied, "I know it's longer than usual, but don't be afraid of it." TWSS

I was in art history class when for some reason the class got on a tangent talking about lobster. Our teacher, who is a monk, apparently hates lobster, because when we asked him whether or not he cared for it, he said, "You would have to either get me really drunk or pay me a lot of money to get me to put that in my mouth." TWSS

Today in our jazz band rehearsal, my professor asked our bass player, "Are you using the one or two finger attack?" TWSS

In concert band one day, a sophomore clarinet had a solo in a song that consisted of some really high notes. After she messed up a few times, the band teacher looked at her and asked what was wrong. The girl replied, "I can't! It's so hard and my mouth is starting to hurt!" TWSS

In science today we were complaining to our teacher that her pencil sharpener is horrible. My friend Rachel exclaimed, "It only takes the skinny ones, too. Every time I try putting a bigger one in that tiny hole the entire thing gets jammed!" TWSS

Today our teacher was telling us how to use a video camera when she said, "You can't just go in and pull out. You gotta stay there for a while. Also, keep it steady, nothing is worse than shaking. You may think you are doing a good job, but people don't like it." TWSS

In art class we were making plaster hands. We had to take turns putting the plaster on somebody else's hand and then they would put it on ours. I was putting plaster on my friend's hand, trying to work slowly and carefully, when suddenly my friend started screaming, "Hurry up! It's getting hard! It's getting hard!" I responded, "I'm trying! But it's getting all over my hands!" TWSS

In biology class, I am the sole girl in a group with three boys. Most groups only have three people. We were doing a really hard lab and none of us could do it right so my lab partner said, "OK, this is gonna be very hard with four people, so who would like to suck first?" TWSS

My friend asked me how I did on my French midterm. I got a good grade because it was a speaking exam and my spoken French is strong. So I replied, "I'm good at oral." TWSS

In orchestra, sometimes we write in numbers over notes to remind ourselves which finger to use on the violin for each note. The best violinist in our class sometimes helps us determine which fingers to use. Our orchestra teacher wisely said, "If any of you need a good fingering, John would be happy to help." TWSS

A girl in my English class was talking about how everyone made fun of her. She said, "Every day I get rode on. First thing in the morning, I wake up and someone's riding on me, and it's not just guys either, girls too. I get rode on long and hard and they just won't stop. I'm just tired of being ridden on while I'm not ready." TWSS

My friend texted me to ask if I had finished reading our reading assignment. I replied, "Yeah, Pedro and I did it last night, but I'm not sure if it counted because he fell asleep half way through. I just kept going, though, because I needed to get it done." TWSS

During math class we had to measure a certain distance with our fingers because we had no rulers. My friend raised his hand and asked the teacher, "Wait, how many fingers do I use for this?" My teacher replied, "Well, I normally use three, but whatever you want." TWSS

We were going to watch a video in class and we were having trouble getting the video into the VCR. Finally, out of frustration, our teacher said, "Just shove it in as hard as you can!" TWSS

One day, this one guy was holding a pen in front of my friend's face and kept moving it just out of her grasp when she went to grab it. She said, "It's just not fair. He keeps dangling it in my face and he just won't give it to me!" TWSS

Today I was watching a dinosaur movie in biology and the woman who was narrating the movie said, "It won't go deeper because it's so big." TWSS

During lunch at school, we noticed that one of our friends was missing, so my friend asked, "Where is he?" Right after she spoke he showed up. My other friend said, "You just had to open your mouth and then he came." TWSS

I was in chemistry class and we were doing a lab with pennies. We had to take some iron wool and try to make the penny shiny. My lab wasn't working out so well, so my teacher came up to me and said, "You're doing it wrong, you have to push hard and make sure you get in there deep." TWSS

We were reading a play in English class and our teacher was trying to get us to pick roles to read. Only the lead characters remained when she announced, "Okay, I need two large male parts!" TWSS

I was at school and one of my friends went to sharpen his pencil. He tried to do it and then he said, "It's not working." My teacher replied, "You just need to stick it in there real good." TWSS

I go to a Catholic high school, which means that sometimes priests will come in to teach us. In English class one day, one of the priests was talking about a story and said, "It starts out soft but then gets hard and long and gives you a great ride." TWSS

My friend was in math class and was trying to get some gunk out of a button on her calculator. When the teacher asked her what she was doing, she replied, "I'm just trying to get this sticky stuff out of my hole." TWSS

I was walking into class with my earbud headphones dangling. A girl exclaimed, "It's dragging on the floor!" TWSS

Today we were in gym class. We were in the locker room and my best friend was trying to put on her shoe. She got upset because her foot couldn't get into the shoe. After about a minute she screamed (really loudly), "It won't go in! Either it's too big or the hole is too small!" TWSS

My friend and I were walking to lunch, and she wanted me to go with her to her locker, so she pulled on my sweater. I said, "No, you're gonna stretch it." She replied, "I'll stretch it until you come." TWSS

Today we were doing a science experiment in class. The experiment was to see which gum can blow the biggest bubble. While my friend was blowing the bubble she said, "It's too soft to blow!" My other partner said, "Once it gets harder, it's easier to blow." Once my friend succeeded in blowing the bubble, she said aloud, "Damn! I'm a good blower!" TWSS

I was in my English class the other day. We had just finished the written portion of a test when my teacher said, "Hand in your papers and we'll start the oral portion." My friend then yelled out, "But I'm not good at oral!" TWSS

Today in art class I was walking up to the table to grab some glue when the teacher said, "Watch the tip, it tends to squirt!" TWSS

One day at school we had two tests. My friend took them before me, so she warned me, "Mr. Colby's was really long and hard, but Mr. Morris's was short." TWSS

My teacher was talking about the final exam. When someone asked if the test was hard, my teacher said, "It's long but not hard." TWSS

In art class we were watching a glass-blowing video. My teacher got up and said, "Look at the size of the things they're blowing! It's huge!" TWSS

In gym class today we played basketball and my teacher said, "Go play with those balls. In the meantime, I will blow all these balls and try to make them hard." TWSS

Today in Latin class, we had a test. My teacher took out the test and said, "Wow, it's so short it's embarrassing!" TWSS

I was trying to take a nap during science class while my teacher was giving a lecture. When he saw me sleeping, he came over to me, woke me up, and said, "We are never going to get this done if you keep falling asleep." TWSS

While sitting at a table in the cafeteria, I was playing with my friend's keys and jokingly threatened to use her pepper spray. She freaked out and said, "If you squirt that in my face we are no longer friends." TWSS

A guy was giving a speech in English class. He rehearsed it before, but it was still under the minimum time limit. In anger, he exclaimed, "It's shorter than I remember!" TWSS

During the after party for a college play, my friend told me she was getting the early signs of a throat infection. She said, "I can feel it in the back of my throat." TWSS

In gym class today we got punished and had to go into push-up, squat, and sit-up position. My friend poked me and whispered, "Man, I really wish he could stop changing positions. I'm starting to get really sweaty and I was starting to get used to the last one!" TWSS

Someone in class gave the teacher a nickname that she didn't like, and she said, "I've had much better ones before." TWSS

My chemistry teacher was explaining how although a meter and a yard are close in length, they are not interchangeable. To illustrate, she held up a yardstick in front of her and said, "You can't just whip it out and be like, this is a meter." TWSS

I was walking into physics and the substitute teacher for the day was talking to a girl there. All I heard the girl say was, "It was nowhere near as big as he said it was." TWSS

In my biology lab today we were doing an experiment that involved using a pipette to insert a solution into a small well submerged in another liquid. It was important when using the pipette not to let go of the plunger until the tip was out of the solution so that you wouldn't draw any more in. To describe this, my lab partner said, "Put it all the way in, but be sure not to release until you've pulled out." TWSS

Today in technology class while plugging our laptops back in, someone yelled, "Ugh! I always put it in the wrong hole!" TWSS

We were doing a science experiment and the teacher said, "You stick it in and take it out. The second time is going to be harder. When you take it out the second time it may be sticky and wet, so don't play with it. Then the third time it will be smooth, slick, and easy to take out." TWSS

In my cooking class my teacher was whipping egg whites. She explained to us, "The stiffer it is, the better." TWSS

At School

Today in my orchestra class my music teacher was explaining to the cello section where to lay their fingers on the fingerboard to make it easier to transition from higher to lower notes faster. When he finished he said, "Now that's some good fingering." TWSS

Today my history teacher was talking about a new computer chair he'd purchased. When one of my classmates asked him how he liked it, he replied, "It's big enough to satisfy me now." TWSS

Today in English class, my teacher was giving a description of the new book we're going to read. She said, "It turns me off because it's so thick, but it's still pretty good." TWSS

I was turning my desk in English and, in the process, hit my friend in the butt with it. She then screamed, "Ow, don't stick that up my butt. That hurts!" TWSS

The other day, I was sitting in the school library with my two friends, a girl and a guy. My female friend had a sore throat, so she said to my male friend, "Do you have anything I can suck on?" TWSS

In my high school music class, we were going over some songs for a concert a few days away. Once we finished one song, our music teacher told us to start another song. A boy shouted, "Oh come on!" to which the teacher replied, "Oh don't you 'come on' me!" TWSS

I was reading my social studies essay out loud to my class. I got to my second paragraph, which read: "The Trojans were stronger and safer than ever." TWSS

All the girls in our year were together in P.E. the other day. My friend threw the ball at a girl and the teacher shouted, "No way mate, that was too fast, she didn't even finish!" TWSS

Today the SMART Board in my math class was not working, so the teacher said, "I guess we'll have to do it orally." TWSS

My chemistry teacher has a very old TV and VCR. One day we tried watching a video and she didn't know where the cable went. She asked, "Is it in?" and a classmate said, "Yeah, but why is it that color? I don't think it's in the right hole." My teacher replied, "I just don't think it's in far enough, it's probably worn out after all these years." TWSS

Today, during a trombone feature, our band director told the trombone section, "More! Keep giving me more until I beg you to stop!" TWSS

My professor was passing around his USB thumb drive to distribute some files. I was about to eject the device on Windows, but he yanked the drive out before it was finished. I said, "You pulled out too soon." TWSS

My friends and I were at lunch at school. We were talking about people shaving their heads and how everyone was doing it. Then my friend said, "I'd shave it for you, Bo." TWSS

Once in English class we had a free day where we didn't have to do any work, so I just knelt by a desk talking to some friends. By the time class was over, my knees were sore, so I said, "Man, my knees hurt from spending so much time on them." TWSS

A couple of friends and I were going to an event at our school. One of my friends was given money by another friend so that he could buy tickets to get into the event. While in the parking lot, he said to us, "I didn't care if I came or not. As long as he's paying." TWSS

Today in gym class a girl was talking about having kinks in her neck and how she gets rid of them. I entered the conversation just in time to hear her say, "I don't do it very often, only when it's really tight." TWSS

At School

I was walking home from school with my friends. It was cloudy and had rained earlier, and one of my friends asked if we could walk faster so we wouldn't get caught by the rain. I replied, "It's not even wet yet, and you wanna go faster?" TWSS

In English class we had to do a summer reading project. I did a PowerPoint presentation and a couple of days later I got my grade back. As my teacher handed it to me, she said, "Everything was great, but your oral presentation didn't satisfy me enough." TWSS

Today, in band rehearsal, our conductor was explaining something to us while I was quietly playing my clarinet. This guy next to me said, "Stop blowing on it." I replied, "I'm not blowing anymore! I'm fingering!" TWSS

Today the whole school had to sit on the basketball courts in the hot sun, and my friend turned to me and said, "Oh fuck, I can't take this, it's hurting my butt." TWSS

I was in science class watching a science lab safety video. The video explained the proper way to put a glass rod into a rubber stopper. It said, "Lubricate the rod before putting it into the hole." TWSS

In our biology class there is a guy who loves to annoy everyone. One day he was sitting behind this girl and he started shaking the back of her seat with his legs. The girl told the teacher that he was shaking the chair and the teacher told her to deal with it. The girl replied, "But he's doing it so hard and fast!" TWSS

I went to a school acting showcase. The teacher told us to put away our cell phones because he thought it was rude. Right after he said that, I blurted out, "Just for that, I'm gonna whip it out and play with it." TWSS

In geography class my teacher announced, "We're doing oral presentations today." My friend said, "Yes, I'm good at oral!" TWSS

My teacher asked this kid to pull a piece of paper out of a jar and read what it said. The kid told my teacher that he couldn't reach in far enough to get to the paper, and my teacher responded, "Keep trying. It's had a lot of fingers in it before." TWSS

My math teacher was telling us about a purchase he made when he lived in Egypt. He said, "I have a lamp that's supposed to have a genie in it. I keep rubbing it but nothing ever comes out." TWSS

I was at drama rehearsal for my school play. The play involves several gods, each of whom has to hold a staff resembling whatever they are a god of. While the teacher was explaining where the gods would stand on their platforms, she said, "There should be a hole right around here where you can stick the staff in. Hopefully it fits." TWSS

At Work

Don't Worry, She's a Professional

My fiancée is a public defender, and she told me about a client she had who she really liked and knew was innocent. She told me, "I am going to do all I can to get this guy off." TWSS

I was at a celebratory lunch with my manager,
director, and eight other coworkers. Several of
them ordered the special, which was a stuffed
cheeseburger. When our food arrived, a woman at
our table said she didn't know how she was supposed
to eat it because of the size. My manager replied,
"You have to unhinge your jaw to get it all in." TWSS

While on the grill line at McDonald's, I took out a
wrapper for the cheeseburger that had appeared
on our order screen. The person working next to
me also took one out and placed it on the counter. I
said, "What are you doing?" He replied, "Oh, I didn't
know you pulled it out already." TWSS

At Work

I am a school bus driver and on my bus there is a two-way radio for communicating with other drivers and base. One morning I heard one driver say to another, "Oh, I'm sorry, I thought you were still inside." TWSS

I was working at Wal-Mart and we were unloading pallets of frozen food off a truck and pulling them to the freezers. Upon reaching the freezer, the female department manager looked at me and said, "He's already in there. Once he pulls his out, you can put yours in." TWSS

Anytime I use my corporate credit card I have to put the receipt in our bookkeeper's mailbox. When she sees me putting a receipt in her mailbox she often jokes that I'm spending too much money. One time she didn't see me putting the receipt in, so when she found it she came out holding it and said, "Go ahead and stick it in there when I'm not looking. It won't make it hurt any less!" TWSS

Today at work a girl made one of those small bags of popcorn. A coworker sitting next to me leaned over and said, "I can't believe it's so tiny." TWSS

A coworker of mine was getting over a cold and had to blow her nose a lot. Before going into a meeting she was blowing her nose and I told her in a joking manner to blow it all out now because there will be none of that for the next hour or so. She responded by saying, "Oh, I will blow, and you will sit there and enjoy it." TWSS

My friend was talking about when dentists inject Novocain into your mouth before working on a cavity, and she said, "It hurts a lot the first time it goes in, but it's a lot less painful the second time, and the third time you hardly feel it at all." TWSS

My friend and I were shooting a short film with several other actors. One girl asked what my friend, the director, wanted her to do. My friend replied (referring to a prop she was holding), "Oh, you can just sit there, look down, and play with your stuff." The actress replied, "That doesn't sound hard at all. Good thing I've done this before." TWSS

We were resetting our office cell phones and one of my coworkers needed a pin or paperclip. When asked what size she needed, her response was, "Anything that will fit in this hole." When she looked at the pin someone gave her, she said, "Oh, that's not going to be big enough." TWSS

I got a summer job mowing lawns. I worked at this one old lady's house, and when I went to her house for the first time she said to me, "Make sure you mow my lawn good. I like it short so it looks good. I want my husband to be proud when he comes home." TWSS

I was talking to a customer on the phone about where she wants to sit in the theater where I work. She said, "Well, my husband is pretty big, and I want him to be able to get in and out pretty easily." TWSS

I was at work yesterday helping load a bunch of supplies into an elevator to take down to the first floor. The girl who was maneuvering the cart lined it up parallel to the elevator, and I said, "That is at the worst possible angle to get it in there." TWSS

I was at work and my boss had just taken his lunch out of the microwave. As he was walking to his office one of my coworkers walked in and said, "Boy, I sure hope that tastes better than it smells." TWSS

I asked my coworker why he was wearing his safety glasses to mix up the chemicals from one bottle with another. He replied, " 'Cause if it gets in my eyes it burns." TWSS

I was at work making a sign and the required length and height had me piecing pages together to finish it. So I said to my coworker, "I keep trying to tell them that if they want it bigger than 8 1/2 inches, it won't work as well!" TWSS

We work in a medical facility, and we had to go in to work on a patient. The medical assistant, having just finished eating a bunch of almonds and cashews, said, "Hold on, let me drink something first so I can wash the taste of all these nuts out of my mouth." TWSS

A girl was at the library printing a cover page for her work. Once it was printed, she picked it up, looked at it, and said, "It's smaller than I thought it would be." TWSS

I was at work and a coworker and I were trying to fit this piece of plywood onto a section of a wall. After having some difficulty, my coworker said, "You can try and stick it in there, but it's going to get really tight." TWSS

While at work, I was trying to get something out of the back of a high drawer. I stood on my tiptoes and stretched, and still couldn't reach it. Frustrated about my height, I turned to my boss and exclaimed, "What I wouldn't give for another half inch!" TWSS

I work for the Census Bureau and today we were assembling binders. We were having a bit of a problem with the hole-punchers and aligning the paper holes with the binder rings when my coworker said, "Why can't I slide it in?" TWSS

My coworker was eating an orange, and she was explaining how she does it. She said, "I like to stick it in my mouth, suck all the juice out, and spit it back out." TWSS

I was at work today when I heard a customer in the other aisle talking to her friend about a beverage she consumed earlier. I heard her say, "It was good, but it left a weird taste in my mouth." TWSS

A girl at my mom's work was trying to help a customer fix his order. After she brought the new order out she said, "If you need anything else, finger me and I'll come." TWSS

At work today someone set up a pair of soccer nets in the office. A female colleague walked around the corner and, surprised by the nets, said, "Oh my God! Where are the balls?" TWSS

The manager was called up to the front of the store to cut a key. She walked up there and said, "I've never done anything that small before." TWSS

At work, we all have mailboxes. My boss was leaving on vacation and said, "Don't put anything in my box!" TWSS

I was drinking coffee at the office and a girl from my department said, "Hey, that thing in your hand is dripping." TWSS

My manager was complaining about having to walk through a downpour on his way in to the building. He said, "I'm still wet from this morning!" TWSS

I was at work and my manager was talking to me and another guy about who'd get to take their break first. She said to me, "You got on first, so you can go first." TWSS

I work in a fast-food restaurant. A car pulled up and they asked for a second to decide what to order. I said sure, then listened in to their conversation. I heard someone in the car say, "Man this is so long . . . I can't fit it all in." TWSS

I was on a ladder at work grabbing pillows off the top shelf and tossing them down to my coworker below. He kept telling me to throw them faster, and so as I started to speed up, I said, "Having fun down there?" TWSS

I was at work with one of my friends and we got the job of refilling the drink coolers. We were joking around and one of the cases of bottles fell. She picked up one that was fizzy and it splashed all over. I yelled, "Oh God, it squirted all over my face!" TWSS

A coworker was pushing a cart through the library. She rammed a table and a shelf and said, "I'm always banging something." TWSS

We were working on a huge computer code today. My buddy looked at me after getting confused yet again, leaned back, and said, "I'm going to just close my eyes, lean back, and wait for you to finish." TWSS

I was at the Verizon Wireless counter when the guy asked me, "So what do you want your phone to be able to do?" I replied, "I just want it to vibrate hard enough so that I can feel it no matter what." TWSS

I worked at a restaurant, and one of our duties was washing dishes. One of my friends started splashing the plates in the water, and finally the manager next to him yelled, "Travis! Knock it off. You got me wet, now finish already." TWSS

When talking to my boss today, I told her that I may need more days than expected for vacation. I hadn't yet put it into the "request-off" book and other people were already requesting similar time off, so she told me, "Make sure you put it in soon or I'll cut it off." TWSS

In pathology today, after seeing a rather large, inflamed gallbladder, one girl exclaimed: "Wow! That thing is huge, there is no way that would ever fit inside my body!" TWSS

I was working at a pizza place today and the lady on the phone said, "I need a twelve-inch Italian Stallion." TWSS

At Work

I was at the dentist getting my second tooth pulled out and he was using the hose to get all the stuff out of my mouth. When he finally stopped, I said, "It's about time you took that goddamn thing out of my mouth. That lasted even longer than last time, and it hurt more, too." TWSS

I was at work at my local grocery store. It just so happened to be a busy day and we were short on people sacking groceries, so some of the managers had to step in. One of them came to my register and started sacking. She looked up at the customer and asked, "Is it okay if I put your sausage in here, sir?" TWSS

I work at a restaurant as a dishwasher. At the end of the night I was washing dishes with a big hose-like faucet. This girl who decided we were going to work together came over and said, "How about I rub and you squirt?" TWSS

I work for a rental car company and we were told to go to the airport and pick up cars for another location. When we got there we radioed back to find out what specific cars to pick up, and the girl on the other end replied, "At least midsize, but the bigger they are, the better I like them." TWSS

My friend and I were unloading a truck of supplies at work. I saw that the hand truck he was loading was full, so I pushed a new one up next to him. He looked at me and said, "Ah, right in the spot where I needed it to come." TWSS

A coworker and I were fixing a toilet paper rack in the men's room at work. We put in the screws and tried to get the rack on without success. Before I could think, I said, "This thing just won't go in," to which my coworker responded, "Maybe we should switch positions." TWSS

A friend and I were using cement to lay bricks, and she said, "Isn't this supposed to be getting hard?" TWSS

At Work

I was working at a Habitat for Humanity demolition site where we were clearing out cement blocks and pieces of wood. One girl stood up and complained, "I'm so tired of bending over!" TWSS

Today after having lunch with a coworker, she got up to throw away both of our plates. When she got back from the garbage can she said, "We almost had a problem. I didn't think the hole was big enough." TWSS

My boss bought a seven-inch TV to watch the Super Bowl on. While looking at it he said, "Wow, seven inches is bigger than I thought." TWSS

I overheard two coworkers in the break room. One was having trouble with the vending machine, but finally got her snack out. The other said, "I was waiting for you to stick your hand up in there." TWSS

My dad is an exercise therapist. I was at his work helping him with some things and he was taking care of a client. He asked her, "How are you doing in this position?" She replied, "It feels so good!" He said, "Awesome. Now just keep doing what you're doing and we'll be done in a minute!" TWSS

I got a pop-up from my antivirus software that asked me if I wanted to renew it. I clicked no, and then I got a second pop-up that asked me, "Are you sure you want to continue unprotected?" TWSS

I was working at a restaurant and was carrying a full load of dishes back to the dish pit. I was saying, "Full load. Full load," so everyone would move. After I set all the dishes down, a girl walked by and said, "Wow, that *is* a big load!" TWSS

At Work

A coworker of mine is always bringing food from these Mexican markets to work. The other day she gave me a piece of Mexican hard candy to try. I asked her how to eat it and she said, "I just put the whole thing in my mouth and suck on it." TWSS

I was telling a friend about how my dentist likes to make small talk while cleaning my teeth. I said, "It's so awkward. I hate how he always tries to have a conversation with me while he's in my mouth." TWSS

Gets Wet

Bodies of Water and Wet Bodies

My friend's cousin was talking to her the other day about a water bottle. Her cousin said, "I took it out of my mouth and it sprayed all over me." TWSS

* * *

A group of friends and I were on Bourbon Street in the middle of a terrible rainstorm that had been going on for hours. It was so bad that there was over a foot of standing water flooding the streets and sidewalks. A girl in the group said, "I've never been this wet before." TWSS

The other day at my lifeguarding job we were opening the pool back up after break and Jon yelled at me to blow my whistle. I told him I don't have one, and he said to use Kevin's. I replied, "I don't wanna blow Kevin's! I have no idea where that thing's been!" TWSS

I had just gotten out of the shower and I took my belly button ring out to clean it. While I was putting it back in I said, "Wow! It goes in easier when it's wet!" TWSS

One day at swim practice, I blew water out of my mouth and created mist. My friend asked how I did that and I replied, "You just get a little in your mouth, and be sure to blow really hard." TWSS

My sailing instructor was teaching us how to keep our boat flat in high winds. She told us, "If you spread your legs, you get more leverage." TWSS

Some friends and I decided to have a water gun fight. I ended up shooting one of them right in the face with my Super Soaker and apparently some of it got up his nose. He said, "Come on! If it had gone in my mouth I wouldn't have cared, but you had to shoot it up the wrong hole!" TWSS

I was drinking out of one of those water bottles that you can squirt into your mouth. Well, I kind of choked on the water. I said to my friend, "I couldn't swallow it! It kept squirting down my throat!" TWSS

Today my friend and I were sitting on the porch looking at this cool tree while it was raining. We were talking about the crack down the middle of it when she said, "It looks better when it's all wet." TWSS

In woodshop class today we were painting some bookshelves. The teacher said very loudly, "You need a wet finish." TWSS

I was at a pool party and there was a slide going into the pool. Someone in the pool told the girl at the top to slide down. The girl replied, "Well, I would need to wet it down before I slide down it." TWSS

Gets Wet

My sister jumped in our pool with a noodle and was
shooting water at everyone with it. She said, "Aww! I
was about to blow and it got all in my hair!" TWSS

I was at my parents' house and we were
all playing volleyball in the pool. One of my
mom's friends held the ball underwater and
let it go so it flew up out of the water. She
screamed and said, "I wasn't expecting it to
shoot up in my face like that!" TWSS

My best friend and I were in the car driving around
on a summer night and it was raining. I had noticed
that she had the window down. I said, "Aren't
you getting wet?" She replied, "Yeah, but it feels
good." TWSS

I was river rafting, and we were going to pass an oar
boat. It was awfully close, and I was sure we were
going to get hit by one of the huge oars. I asked the
guide and she said, "Oh don't worry, when they see
you coming they pull it out." TWSS

Today at swim practice my coach shouted at me: "KEVIN! Stop slapping it like that! Just smoothly slide it in!" TWSS

My friend brought a water bottle on the bus and squirted it on some girls in the front. They yelled, "You got it all over my face and in my hair. Stop spraying all over me!" TWSS

While I was lifeguarding this guy came up and asked for a Band-Aid. I asked him what size he wanted. He said, "Oh, it doesn't matter, the longer the better." TWSS

My friends and I were filling up water balloons when my friend's balloon exploded and she said, "Oh my gosh, I wasn't even holding it that tight and it exploded all over me." I replied, "Next time stop before it gets too big, then it won't explode." TWSS

I was in my percussion class and the teacher was showing us the hand position. He got angry at a kid who wouldn't tighten his fulcrum and he said, "No, no, take it, grip it, slide it in, then start pushing. No! No! That's too hard! Slide it in! Slide it in! Yes, yes, that's it! Slide, slide, okay." He gestured to his sweating hands. "I think you're getting a little too wet, now." TWSS

My friend and I were on vacation at the beach and a big wave crashed into us. She said, "Wow, I didn't know what to expect and then it just came on my face." TWSS

I was playing beer pong with my friend. I picked the ball up off the floor and said, "Did it go in? Because it's awfully wet." TWSS

Today at water polo practice my coach was explaining a drill where we pass with two balls. We were all in the shallow end and he said, "Let's try going deeper. Just make sure to keep track of both balls and keep gripping them!" TWSS

At lunch my friend squeezed her juice box too hard and said, "I felt it squirt all over my face." TWSS

One of my teachers was talking to me about the track meet I was going to be running in that night. It had been raining and he said, "Looks like you're going to get wet tonight." TWSS

For agriculture class we have to take measurements outside with a measuring tape. One day it was raining and the tape wouldn't go back inside like it's supposed to. My friend said, "Just put it in already, I'm getting wet!" TWSS

We were sitting in the computer room the other day when my sister decided to get a gallon of water. She explained to us how she was going to drink it without spilling a drop and said, "I'm going to put my mouth on it and suck it dry." TWSS

My brother, my friend, and I were in the Jacuzzi and my brother splashed my friend with water. She said, "Eww, it got in my mouth!" TWSS

My friend and I were playing with a Super Soaker squirt gun. My friend's gun wasn't squirting far, so my mom came over and said, "You have to pump it long and hard so there is enough pressure for it to squirt." TWSS

During class today we were presenting commercials and a guy did his for a water park. At the end of his commercial, he said, "Be sure to bring your towels, it's going to be a wet night." TWSS

The other day I had my reed in my mouth before music class. A friend asked me why I had it in my mouth. I replied, "It has to be wet before you play with it." TWSS

I was camping with my friend and we went to go fill up a jug with water from the pump. She pumped the water while I held the jug underneath the tap. The jug slipped slightly in my hands, causing water to spray at me. I said to my friend, "Ugh, you got it all over me!" To which she responded, "It's not my fault! You pulled out too fast!" TWSS

I was having a water gun fight with my friend. I had pretty bad aim and accidentally aimed too high. She ended up screaming, "You know I hate it when you squirt me in the eye!" TWSS

I saw a new gum commercial that said, "It's the wettest thing in the world." TWSS

My friends and I were at church waiting for youth group to start when one of my friends fell into a puddle. Another friend said to him, "Why is it every time you come, you get wet?" TWSS

My friend was looking at a picture of herself with a guy friend. The photo was of them coming back from a theme park. I remarked that they looked really soaked and sweaty. She said, "Don't make fun of me, he just got me so wet on that last ride." TWSS

We were playing with squirt guns and while my friend was filling one up, he took the hose and got everyone all wet. My friend said, "You took it out way too early and I'm sooooo wet! Put it back in and don't get it everywhere!" TWSS

I was at lunch and my friend was drinking lemonade. All of a sudden he spilled it all over everyone. Someone said, "Wow, you got me all wet and sticky." TWSS

Our swim coach was always yelling at us for being too slow and easy when we came off the blocks. He gave us a lecture the other day in which he said, "You have to go in hard and come out wet and breathless. You'll feel good when you're done." TWSS

It had been raining for hours one night and all of my friends and I were completely soaked. On the way back from the bars we were casually walking in the downpour and having fun in the water. When we passed people huddled together under awnings trying to stay dry, my friend yelled to them, "You need to get wet!" TWSS

During lunch my friend wanted some water from someone else's water bottle, but didn't want to drink directly from it, so he said, "Just squirt it in my mouth, but make sure you aim. I don't want it to get all over my face." TWSS

Gets Wet

My friend and I had been playing outside in a short rainstorm. When it was over, my friend said that it had been fun. I replied, "It was exciting, I just wish it would've lasted longer." TWSS

Goes Wild

She's a Dirty Girl

I was showing my friend a picture of an Irish Greyhound because she was interested in dogs and she said, "Too big, I could ride that thing like a horse." TWSS

My cousin's girlfriend was smelling flowers in a lilac bush. After spending a few moments inhaling, she turned around and said, "This bush smells so good, I just want to keep my face in it all day." TWSS

Today my campers were learning how to cut wood. One camper's ax got stuck and a fellow leader said, "If it gets stuck, don't worry. Just wiggle it a little, and it will come out." TWSS

We were collecting sticks to make a fire at camp and my friend found heaps of sticks. She distributed them to some of the guys. Later she said, "If it weren't for me half these guys wouldn't even have wood." TWSS

My dad was watching a TV show about crabs. I walked into the room and all I heard was, "OK guys, this thing is big and it's super hard. So what we're going to do is hover right over it, tackle it, and then lower ourselves onto it until it sprays. Got it?" TWSS

We were in meteorology class discussing thunderstorms. Our professor explained that "In the mature stage is when we get wet and see some action." TWSS

I went on a long, muddy hike with a friend not long ago. Each of us attracted our share of leeches. When we returned, she took off her shoe and saw a giant leech attached to her foot. She promptly let out quite the scream and said, "Sorry I squealed, that was the biggest one I've seen in a long time." TWSS

I was at a summer camp. They were handing out rings for everyone; there were black rings for the boys and yellow for the girls. The black ones were made to fit a boy's finger and the yellow ones were made to fit a girl's finger. My friend asked me to get him one and he said, "Get me a black one. The black ones are always bigger." TWSS

We were watching the forecast and I was in a different room, so my sister relayed it to me: "Getting pounded by a swift and smooth snowstorm, approximately ten inches. Seventy-five percent chance of definite whiteout conditions. There'll be a huge amount of white semi-liquid substance everywhere once the activity has finished near midnight. Maybe even missing work tomorrow from getting hit so hard." TWSS

Today I was playing manhunt with some of my friends. I hid in my neighbor's bush on her lawn. She was upset and yelled, "Get out of my bush, you little bastard, I just trimmed it!" TWSS

Goes Wild

I was watching a video where this guy went
to India and rode on an elephant. He said,
"You know, I really feel like there is something
powerful between my legs." TWSS

I was sitting in the living room with my friend and a bee
was buzzing around the room. Then my friend covered
her mouth and said, "I shouldn't yell or it might come in
my mouth." TWSS

I was bowling with my friends yesterday
and a news update came on about
hurricane Alex. Before the reporter finished
talking about the storm she said, "It's big,
it's slow, and it's gonna be long." TWSS

This weekend I went to the beach with my family.
While we were putting sunscreen on, my sister
turned to me and said, "Is there any white stuff on my
face?" TWSS

One night a friend came back to my dorm all excited that she had found a potato bug outside. She had caught it in a cup and as she was showing it to us exclaimed, "I touched it and it was all hard!" TWSS

Today I was hiking with my brother-in-law and a couple passed us while talking about the trailheads. The woman said to the man, "You have to pay to use the front entrance, but the rear entrance is no charge. I prefer using that one; it's more fun." TWSS

I was planting trees with some friends for a summer job. The trees needed to be put in specific spots. We dug the holes and were about to put one tree in when a friend said, "Not that hole you idiot! The other one!" TWSS

I was petting my cat's tummy and he stretched out farther than I've ever seen and I said, "Wow, I didn't know he could get that long!" TWSS

Goes Wild

My neighbor came over to my house tonight to hang out and we got to talking about my dogs. One of my dogs' kennels has a hole chewed in it from a time we left the dogs home during a thunderstorm. Noting the growing size of the hole in the dog's kennel, my neighbor exclaimed, "Of course it's getting bigger, you keep sticking stuff in the hole!" TWSS

While I was walking with friends we saw a large dog with its owner. The dog was dragging the person across the sidewalk. One of my friends said, "Wow, that's a really big dog." My other friend said, "I guess so, but I've seen bigger." TWSS

Today my mom and I went to a gardening store. We bought a huge bag of soil for the plants in the backyard. I didn't think it would fit in the trunk, so I said to my mom, "It's not going to fit." She replied, "Come on, if you turn it the other way it will fit." I said, "You're right, it's smaller than it looks. I thought it was bigger." TWSS

Last night, an earthquake hit Southern California. My friend called me to describe the quake: "Yeah, it was a big scary one. I was shaking, it lasted so long!" TWSS

My friend and I were going on a camping trip with her family and had to stop at Wal-Mart to get some extra things. When we were getting ready to go inside, his mom said, "We have to make this a quickie, in and out." TWSS

My friend, telling me about the time she swallowed a fly, said, "It was long and black and wouldn't get out of me. It was coming at me so fast I didn't have time to close my mouth. That thing entered so quickly." TWSS

The other day, I was at the beach, and a lady near me was trying to get sunblock out of the bottle. All of a sudden I heard her say, "I just squirted everywhere!" TWSS

Goes Wild

I was talking to my wife on the phone and she mentioned that she had just taken our dog out in the middle of a rainstorm. Concerned his wet fur would ruin the furniture, I told her not to let him on the couch. She replied, "Don't worry, I blew him dry." TWSS

Hits the Road

She Really Gets Around

Today my friend was driving and looking for a parking spot. She was passing a car and the car backed up without warning. She yelled, "Why the fuck would you pull out right when I'm coming?" TWSS

My dad and I were driving past a hardware store when we saw a truck leaving the parking lot with a bunch of two-by-fours in the back. As the truck turned onto the street, the two-by-fours started falling out of the bed. My dad said, "Oh, jeez, that's no good, he hasn't even pulled out yet and he's already losing wood." TWSS

I was in the airport and since I was delayed two hours I was entertaining myself by chewing three pieces of Bubblicious and blowing as big of a bubble as possible. After a while, the gum got a little stale and hard to chew. I said, "This is getting pretty hard and it's hard to blow." TWSS

I was driving with my friend in a tiny parking lot. A car zoomed past us going the other direction. My friend yelled, "You can't go that fast when it's this tight!" TWSS

We were riding in the car with my friend and she was speeding in a 45 mph area. I looked over to my friend in the backseat and said, "Wow, she's such a rebel. She's doing 69 now!" TWSS

My mom and I were in the car driving and it was cold outside. She said she was cold so I turned on the heat. When the hot air came out of the vents she said, "Why does it have to come on my face?" TWSS

Our class writes "snaps" to each other like in the movie *Legally Blonde*. They're one-liners that give thanks or recognition for the week. Earlier in the week my roommate rode with my lead-footed classmate to Wal-Mart and back. My roomie wrote a snap saying, "Snaps to Aaron for giving me the ride of my life in your car." TWSS

I overheard my dad telling my mom how to check the oil level on her car. He told her to, "Pull out the stick, wipe it off, then put it back in. Then pull it out again and look at how much fluid is left on the stick." TWSS

Today I was driving back from the post office and I could see a car down the street ready to pull out in front of me. I said out loud, "Don't pull out! DO NOT PULL OUT!" TWSS

My brother and I were installing something in his car that you had to put in a slot. I put it in without him noticing and he said, "You already put it in? I didn't even know it was in yet." TWSS

I was in the car telling my mom about my friend's plans for his Sweet Sixteen. He wanted to drive a stretch Hummer down to the harbor. Then I stopped to think about that and said, "I don't know how they're going to fit something that big down there." TWSS

Hits the Road

Today my friend and I were waiting for our friend to come pick us up from school to start our road trip to California. My friend was so excited that she was bouncing up and down, saying, "Oh God, ohh God, OH GOD! This is gonna be amazing!" I told her to calm down and she replied, "I can't! He needs to come faster!" TWSS

Driving down the street today my mom decided to speed up to test out her new Infiniti FX35. My sister said, "Wow, Mom, you're going really fast," to which my mom replied, "Yeah, sometimes I like to open her up and play with her." TWSS

My girlfriend and I were driving down the interstate. The road was really bumpy and making both of us vibrate just enough to make it irritating. Pretty soon it started making my seat shake a little and was making my ass vibrate. I turned to her and said, "I can feel it in my butt." TWSS

My buddy and I were in his driveway about to leave for a movie when his mom called. She was driving down his street, and when we told her we were about to leave, she said, "Don't pull out until I come, I'm almost there!" TWSS

We were trying to fit a new TV into the back of my grandma's truck and my mom said, "It's OK, bigger things have been shoved in there." TWSS

This week, my family and I spent a couple of days at a hotel. My sister was having trouble opening the door with the key card, but she refused to let anyone else try, so my mom said, "Put it in really slowly, then yank it out fast." TWSS

A friend and I were driving down the road. He said, "You lost an earring." I reached down my shirt to see if it had fallen down there. He asked if I found it. I replied, "It might be in there, but it's so small I don't feel it." TWSS

My friends and I were driving on the highway to go out for lunch. We were getting close to an off-ramp that was not the one we wanted. I said, "Don't get off yet, keep going!" TWSS

My friends and I were in terrible Los Angeles traffic, with people lining up to get into the clubs on Hollywood Boulevard. We saw this white Hummer limo struggling to switch lanes. My friend noticed this and said, "He's so big, let the poor guy in. It's probably already hard." TWSS

When I was in the car with my brother on the highway, the driver behind us was annoyingly close. My brother glanced in the rearview mirror and said, "Why is he riding my butt so hard?" TWSS

We were on a bus going to our car from the airport and the bus driver said, "My back door is a little sticky, so you can't use that one." TWSS

My guy friends came over one day and we were getting ready to go somewhere. We were planning on going to our favorite café by cab. My mom came into my room and said, "Guys, are you sure that you wanna go like that? I'm free, I have nothing better to do, and I can give each of you a ride if you guys want. Especially you, Michael, you're my favorite." TWSS

My guy was telling me that he had worked on a motorcycle over the weekend. I said, "Are you gonna take me for a ride? I've never been on one." TWSS

My brother was polishing out the scratches on his motorcycle, and when he asked my mother how to get a big scratch out, she said, "Just rub it harder and it will come out." TWSS

My friend and I were getting a ride home, and she called shotgun, so I said, "It's okay, I can handle two minutes in the backseat of a car." TWSS

My best friend was driving through a parking lot when another driver began backing out of her spot. My friend, afraid that she was about to be hit, yelled, "No! Don't pull out while I'm still coming!" TWSS

I was on a flight, and the guy next to me was having trouble with his headphone socket. He called a flight attendant and said, "I can't get any sound." The flight attendant said, "Have you tried taking it out and putting it back in?" To which the guy replied, "Yeah, I put it in all the way. Oh, wait, it's coming now." TWSS

I was in my friend's car and I started to roll the window down because it was hot. He stopped me and said not to because "It goes down easy but it's hard to get it back up." TWSS

I just recently got my driver's license and my sister was talking to me and the rest of my family about when she first started driving: "I remember when Dad asked if I was ready to handle a populated road and I was super excited, but when I came to the intersection, I pulled out too late and a guy came in my ass." TWSS

My friend was bragging about how he gets an awesome parking spot close to the building every morning, despite showing up around the same time as the rest of us. He said, "I just keep going up and down until someone pulls out." TWSS

My friend was sitting in the back of my car trying to buckle her seat belt and she couldn't figure out which one was the right one. My other friend said, "Try to stick it in the other hole." TWSS

I was on the bus listening to my iPod when I heard my friend who was eating a lollipop scream, "Ewww, it's all dirty. I don't wanna lick that." TWSS

Last night my friend's car wouldn't start. She had the key in the ignition, but the key wouldn't turn. I said, "Are you pushing it in far enough? That might be why it's not turned on." TWSS

My friend and I were on a long car ride, and I started to get squirmy in my seat. I told him, "This is starting to hurt my ass. Can we switch positions?" TWSS

My friend and I were trying to find a parking space and we had to park really far away from where we wanted to go. As we were walking to the store, we saw a car leave a space ten feet away from the store. My friend said, "Dammit, you couldn't have pulled out five seconds ago?" TWSS

My friends were meeting at a party, and one friend was on the highway about to approach the exit. My friend said, "Let me know when you're getting off because I want to come at the same time." TWSS

Falling in Love

It's Not You, It's Her

My boyfriend put food in the microwave for five seconds and then took it out. I said, "You can't expect to just put it in, take it out, and it to be finished." TWSS

Right before mini golfing, my date was pretty nervous because he didn't want to suck at it. He said, "It's pretty hard, but I can usually ease myself into the hole." (TWHS) Then he said, "Wow, I really opened myself up for that one." TWSS

I was in math class and this girl came in with something on her shirt, so my teacher asked, "What is on your shirt?" She replied, "My boyfriend squirted something on me." TWSS

I was sitting next to a girl I'm seeing and playing with a Koosh ball. She said, "If you play with it in front of me, I'm going to want to touch it." TWSS

Falling in Love

My girlfriend accompanied me to my friend's house for a game of Halo. Knowing that she liked the aesthetic value of things, I gave her the choice of two controllers. I asked her, "Would you like the black one or the white one?" She answered, "It doesn't matter. I'll suck on both." TWSS

My girlfriend and I had lunch at Subway today. She ordered a six-inch, and I ordered the foot-long. After watching me scarf down the last bite, she asked me, "How do you eat the foot-long? After six inches I'm stuffed!" TWSS

My mom and her boyfriend were talking about Twizzlers. All I heard was: "I like to put the whole thing in my mouth at once. Yeah, that's how I like it." TWSS

Today my girlfriend and I were listening to her iPod on the move. She had her earpiece in and was choosing a song. After selecting a song, she handed me the other piece and said, "Put this in. You'll like it." TWSS

The other day, my dad, his girlfriend, and I went out for dinner. She ordered a burger, and when it came out she said, "This thing is huge. There's no way I'm gonna fit all this in my mouth." TWSS

Today on the bus ride home from school, my friends who are in a relationship were in their normal seat. There was a huge hole in the seat. She said, "Nathan, can you fit your whole fist in there?!" TWSS

Today I was at Burger King. A cute girl came into line behind me. We started chatting and we both ordered chocolate shakes. We got our orders at the same time. The shakes came with unusually large straws and she exclaimed, "Will you look at the size of that thing! I'm never gonna be able to suck anything out of that." TWSS

Today my girlfriend and I were sitting at work. Being bored, I decided to go pull the end of her shoelace, thus untying her shoe. She yelled, "Nooo! Don't pull it out!" TWSS

One day I was sitting at the bowling alley with a few friends. I was busy talking to my boyfriend while my friends were talking about some guy's muscles. All I heard was, "God, it's just so big. And it bulges out there!" TWSS

Today I was making Rice Krispies squares with my girlfriend. She was playing with the marshmallows after they were melted and said, "Oh my, this is sticky!" I said, "Just put it in your mouth. I'm sure it tastes better than it looks." TWSS

My girlfriend and I were making dinner at my mother's. My girlfriend was frying some chicken in the pan. My mom saw it was a lot of chicken and suggested that she fry it in two batches, to which my girlfriend proudly replied, "If there's anything I'm an expert at, it's making things fit into small spaces!" TWSS

School just got out and it was snowing really badly. My sister, her boyfriend, and I were walking to the bus, into the snow, which was blowing right at us. My sister burrowed her face into her boyfriend, so he asked her what was wrong. She replied, "I hate it when it blows in my face!" TWSS

My friend was talking about her new boyfriend and how he's so great. She explained how he understands her, and she said, "He gets so deep. Nobody's ever been that far inside, and it feels so good to just release it all for him." TWSS

Today I was asking if I should write my report for school before my girlfriend wrote hers. She replied, "No, because it will take me longer than you to finish." TWSS

I let my girlfriend drive my truck. When she got back I told her she did a good job not hitting anything. She said, "It's longer than I'm used to, but I handled it okay." TWSS

I was on a date the other night when the guy decided to take me to a sushi restaurant. It was my first time eating sushi. When we got there, he ordered a few tuna rolls, picked one up with his chopsticks, and attempted to feed it to me. Not thinking, I blurted out (loudly), "It's so big! I can't possibly fit the whole thing in my mouth!" TWSS

I was at a restaurant with my boyfriend and I noticed he had a bit of ketchup in the corner of his mouth. I pointed it out to him and he tried to rub it off with his thumb, but it was still there. I said to him, "Just keep licking it and rubbing it. That'll get it off." TWSS

My girlfriend and I were playing slaps when she said, "I'm better on bottom." TWSS

While I was waiting impatiently for my boyfriend to pick me up and take me to the dentist I said, "Can't you come faster? My mouth hurts!" TWSS

Today my boyfriend noticed a hole in my sweater and said, "Did you know you have a little hole right here? Do you ever play with it to make it bigger?" TWSS

I was helping my girlfriend's family move. Her two brothers and I were moving this insanely heavy California king bed and trying to find room in the trailer when one of the brothers said, "Just put it in the crack." TWSS

I was at the bar with my wife and buddies, and we ordered some Washington apple shots. I gave one to my wife, who said, "There's no way I can fit all of this in my mouth!" TWSS

I was decorating my friend's mom's office for her fortieth birthday and my friend was blowing up balloons. She was texting her boyfriend about it and wrote, "I was blowing it 'til it exploded in my face." TWSS

Falling in Love

I was having a texting conversation with an ex-boyfriend and he was explaining something to me. When he finished his explanation he texted me, "Should I go deeper?" I texted him back, "Yes, go deeper." TWSS

My friend was taking clothes out of the dryer and putting newly washed clothes into it. He said, "Damn, I forgot to put the laundry detergent in." His wife replied, "Josh, you could be on your second load if you would have done it right the first time." TWSS

My boyfriend and I were in his room today and he had decided to start playing his guitar. I told him to play a song that he's normally not too good at. About halfway through the song he said to me, "Can I stop this now? It's too hard and my hands are starting to hurt." TWSS

My friend was talking to me about his problems with his girlfriend. He said, "It's hard to get really deep." TWSS

The other day I was about to unload the dishwasher. A measuring cup got turned over, so it had water in it. I yelled, "Holy shit!" My boyfriend asked what happened, and I said, "All I did was pull it out, I didn't even touch it, and it exploded all over my pants!" TWSS

The other day my girlfriend and I took pics on my phone and she asked me to put them on Facebook. For some reason, I wasn't able to post them directly from my phone. I told her and she responded, "Aww, come on. Can't you find a way to put it in?" TWSS

I was eating chili while on the phone with my boyfriend. I took a bite that was bigger than the rest and said, "That was a lot more meat than I thought would fit in my mouth!" TWSS

Falling in Love

I was bartending one night and a guy bought his date several drinks that she just sipped before pushing away. Finally fed up with her pickiness, he ordered an Irish car bomb so she would have to down it. Before she took the shot, he said to her, "Okay you just gotta swallow it fast, 'cause if you let it sit too long in your mouth, it will be too creamy to swallow!" TWSS

I was at my friend's house and we were in her room while her sister and her sister's boyfriend were in the next room. We heard her sister scream, "Oh my God! It's so big and hard and I just wanna touch it." TWSS

My girlfriend was putting her contacts in when she yelled, "It might be a couple of minutes, I can't get it in!" TWSS

My boyfriend and I were washing his car. I was the one with the sponge and soap and he had the hose. My boyfriend sprayed me with the water and I said, "Gosh, you're making me so wet." TWSS

My girlfriend and I were in bed and I tickled her. She jumped up real fast and I said, "That was the fastest I've ever seen you get up." TWSS

My girlfriend was shotgunning a beer at a party. Halfway through, she started choking, so I asked if she was okay. She replied, "I thought I could swallow it all, but I was wrong." TWSS

One day I was at my boyfriend's house with a bunch of friends playing pool. He was counting on his partner to make the last shot to win the game. His partner didn't hit it hard enough, so it stopped right in front of the side pocket. My boyfriend said, "Aww, if it was a little bit harder, it would've gone in." TWSS

My boyfriend, his sister, and I had just gotten home after a movie. She had a cut in her mouth from biting her lip. She went to the bathroom and, as she was looking in the mirror, said, "It looks so small, but it feels so big in my mouth!" TWSS

Falling in Love

I was hanging out with my sister and her boyfriend and we got hungry, so I decided to make a frozen pizza. After the oven was preheated my sister said, "Stick it in, then take it out in twenty minutes." TWSS

In band class, our conductor was talking about how great our co-conductor is. The co-conductor's wife was in the room and said, "He can do magical things with his fingers." TWSS

I was at the house of this girl I was dating and she was telling me about how she had to drink liquid barium to get her upper GI tract looked at by the radiologist. I asked her what it was like and she replied, "Well, it was kind of thick and creamy and it was hard to swallow down. It kept getting stuck in my throat." TWSS

My girlfriend and I were eating some Nerds candy, and she noticed that I was eating them one by one. She said, "I like to just put a whole load in my mouth and suck on it." TWSS

My girlfriend was on her way to pick me up and my sweatshirt was damp, so my mom gestured to the dryer and said, "Stick it in and keep it in 'til she comes!" TWSS

Goes Out to Eat

Eating Out with Her

While buying groceries today the bagger said, "I'm just going to wrap your meat so it doesn't mix with the eggs." TWSS

* * *

My friend and I decided to have a whipped cream eating contest. We used aerosol cans, and halfway through my friend sprayed way too much and said, with her mouth full, "AHH! It exploded in my mouth! But it tastes pretty good!" TWSS

I was baking with my roommate, stirring the dough to keep it from firming while he heated the oven. I asked him if the oven was ready yet, and he replied, "Just keep on beating it. You're not putting it in anytime soon." TWSS

Today I was eating a sub with extra mayonnaise and a girl saw it and said, "It's so big. Look at all the white stuff coming out." TWSS

Goes Out to Eat

My best friend and I had gotten foot-longs from Subway. One half was a bit larger than the other so we saved the smaller piece for later. After a night out, my best friend finished the second half of her sandwich and sent me a text that said, "Best four inches ever." TWSS

On Easter Sunday, my Nana and Auntie came over for lunch. I left the table to get something from my room, and when I came back my Nana was pissing herself laughing and trying to say something. She finally spit it out: "I kept telling him, not that hole, it's too small! Put it in the other hole!" TWSS

A few of my buddies and I were sitting around at a local bar when we heard a knock on the back door. Someone shouted to let them in, and my friend said, "He's not going to be able to get in the back door, there's a stool in the way." TWSS

That's What She Said

This evening my roommate pulled out a
can of whipped cream to put on his yogurt.
After topping it off, he sprayed some into his
mouth. A few seconds later, with his mouth
full, he said, "Man, that was a lot more than I
expected." TWSS

Today at lunch my friend was eating her
hamburger slowly. I got up to leave and was about
midway out of the cafeteria when I noticed she
still hadn't finished yet, so I said, "Just shove it in
and come already!" TWSS

Once, during lunch, a friend of mine spilled something
on her leg and was trying to wipe it off. Another friend
of mine screamed, "Stop, the more you rub it, the more
it comes!" TWSS

My brother was eating something nasty
and we were all making a big deal out of it.
He said, "I regretted it as soon as I put it in
my mouth." TWSS

I was trying to take the cap off of my Strawberry Coolatta from Dunkin' Donuts while I was waiting for my dad to come pick up me and my friend. The top was really difficult to remove, so I said, "I know that as soon as I take my top off, he's going to come." TWSS

During the summer, I went to get a bubble tea with my friend. It was her first time drinking it, so she didn't know that the balls inside were tapioca. The woman behind the counter forgot to give her a straw, so she went up and asked, "Excuse me, how do I suck on these balls?" TWSS

My little cousin had a cup of lemonade and he was trying to put the straw in the lid, and his mom said, "No, honey, not that hole, it's too small. I don't think it will fit, try again." TWSS

My mom was teaching my sister how to cut the skin off of mangoes. My sister accidently cut off way more than just the skin, and she said, "Oops, is that okay?" My mom replied, "That's fine. It's better when you go deep." TWSS

I was at a workshop with some colleagues and we were all really looking forward to lunch, which was a taco bar. As one of my coworkers, Lisa, was getting ready to eat her taco, she got really excited and said, "This is going to be the most amazing thing I've ever put in my body." TWSS

My brother and I were eating at a restaurant. He was having trouble squeezing salsa out of a bottle, so he said, "I hate it when it doesn't come out, because you know it's just going to explode." TWSS

My friend had a small cookie inside a clear plastic wrapper that he didn't want, so he offered it to other people at lunch. My other friend was so excited about the cookie he yelled, "Forget about the wrapper, I want it in my mouth now!" TWSS

Today my brother and mom were making a pie. They took it out of the fridge and my mom said, "You know, I think you took it out too early. Put it back in for a while." TWSS

A group of friends and I were at a Mexican restaurant. When the food arrived one of my friends exclaimed, "There's too much meat in my taco!" TWSS

My sister was heating up a soft pretzel in the microwave, and before she put it in she sprinkled a whole bunch of salt on it. I cautioned her that it may be too much. She replied, "Whatever, if it's too salty, I'll just spit it out." TWSS

Some mates and I were having kebabs the other day, and my one mate who was reasonably inebriated took a bite of his kebab and some of the salad fell out. He said, "There's more on the floor than in my mouth." TWSS

I was at my friend's house for dinner and we had BLTs. While his mom ate her sandwich, mayonnaise oozed out. Noticing this, she said, "It's so juicy. It's running down my face." TWSS

My teammates and I went out to buy fruit shakes and noodles at the grocery store. One teammate ordered a shake that was bigger than her usual size. We told her that we had to take the food to go, so while clutching her wallet and phone in one hand and the noodles in the other, she tried to clench the twenty-two-ounce shake in her hand with the noodles. Unable to bring it with her, she said, "My hands are too small and it's too big. I can't grip it." TWSS

I was sitting at lunch licking the chocolate off a Pocky Biscuit Stick. My friend asked, "Why are you licking it like that?" TWSS

When I used to visit my grandmother, we liked to talk about anything, really. Well, this time we were talking about food—Little Debbie Snacks, more specifically. My grandmother said, "I love the Ding Dongs. They are long and feel amazing when they enter your mouth!" TWSS

I was eating lunch with a few friends. Two of them decided to order one large drink and share it using two straws. As one of them was taking a drink, she lifted the straw out of the cup while still sucking on it. The other screamed, "Don't pull it out yet! You're not finished!" TWSS

My mom, my sister, and I were in the kitchen making smoothies. As my mom was pouring the smoothies, my sister said, "I want the thickest one!" TWSS

I was making sugar cookies with my little sister and I told her to put the cookies on the cooling rack to harden. She exclaimed, "OMG they are already hard, I just want to put it in my mouth right now!" TWSS

My friend was eating a cookie with white frosting inside. While taking a bite she said, "I keep swallowing the white stuff, but it keeps on coming!" TWSS

Our drama club was having its cast party at McAlister's Deli after one of our shows. The waiter was taking our orders when the girl next to me said, "Yes, I'll have mine white and twelve inches. I like the extra meat." TWSS

My aunt had just made some homemade mashed potatoes. They were really hot, so she said, "This is really hot, you want me to blow it for you?" TWSS

I was with my friend and her grandma going to a chocolate store. My friend and I were saying how the chocolates there are warm and melt in your mouth. Her grandma yelled, "Oh, you really gotta put the whole thing in your mouth, or else all the stuff comes out all over ya!" TWSS

I had taken a stick of butter from the fridge and left it out. My mom saw it was starting to melt and she said, "Put it back in so it can get hard again." TWSS

I was camping with a bunch of my friends, and we had honey and pita bread that night for dinner. My friend said, "I love that stuff. Squirt it right in my mouth." I said, "Lean your head back and open wide." She replied, "Okay, don't put too much down my throat, I don't want to choke." TWSS

I was talking to my friend about beer and told her that nine beers will do me. She replied, "Three will do me. I had six once and couldn't walk." TWSS

My very conservative Italian friend brought in cannolis for an end-of-the-year party. As she bit into hers, she exclaimed, "It just burst in my mouth! Now the white stuff is all over my face." TWSS

I made brownies in cooking class today and they had nuts in them. Everyone started to eat them, when one of the girls got pissed and said, "Your nuts are stuck in my throat." TWSS

My friend, her brother, and I were eating whipped cream, when her brother tried to spray some in my mouth. While explaining this to my friends later I said, "He whipped it out, tried to squirt it in my mouth, but he missed and got it all over my face!" TWSS

Today I was babysitting. I took the kids to a restaurant, and the girl was talking about how she takes the lid off of her kid's meal cup: "Once I've been drinking a lot, my top comes off pretty easily." TWSS

One of my friends gave me a huge lollipop today and I started to lick it. I said, "I could suck on this all day! I'm just so good at it." TWSS

My friend was picking up a chocolate bar, and before she put it in her mouth she said, "You want to go in there, don't you big boy?" TWSS

My little brother was watching TV and eating a banana. My mom walked out into the living room and said to him, "Be careful! Don't stick the whole thing in your mouth, it's too big and you'll choke!" TWSS

My mom got a Frosty at Wendy's the other day. It was taking a while for it to come out of the straw, so she said, "Ugh! I keep sucking and sucking and sucking as hard as I can, but nothing is coming out!" TWSS

My friend and I were at a Mexican restaurant. We just received our burritos, when she said, "Oh man, this thing is huge and it's all going to be inside me!" TWSS

My friend and I were having Chick-fil-A at school, and my other friend said that he could eat the whole chicken in one bite. He failed and I said, "What the hell is wrong with you? I couldn't get all that meat in my mouth even if I push it all the way down my throat." TWSS

One day my friend was eating a huge apple. She cried out in excitement, "It's so large and tender! I can barely fit my hands around it!" TWSS

Two guys and four girls were all out eating one night at a Korean BBQ restaurant. One of the guys had trouble calculating his part of the bill. So one of the girls said, "Geez, it's like he's never eaten out before!" TWSS

My friend and I were making a house in art class, and she was using the hot glue gun. I pulled out cookies from my bag, ate one, and offered her one. She said, "My hands are busy, just put it in my mouth." TWSS

My friend Brandi was sitting at our cafeteria table, aimlessly playing with her milk carton. She squeezed it, and the milk gushed out the top and shot to a surprising height. With utter amazement in her voice, she said, "Dude, I squeezed it and it shot up into the air and landed on my face!" TWSS

I took the roast out of the oven, started cutting it, and saw that there was too much blood inside still, so I went to put it back in the oven. My partner said, "Quick, put it back in before it drips everywhere." TWSS

I was at a friend's house and we were eating oranges. She asked if I ate the filmy part around the pulp, and I told her I didn't. She agreed and said, "I just suck on it 'til the juice comes out." TWSS

My girlfriend, my sister, and I were in the kitchen with my grandmother talking about bananas. My sister said, "I don't like bananas because they're mushy." My grandma replied, "I don't like them when they are soft, I like them when they're firm and hard." TWSS

I had put a bottle of wine back into the fridge and after a little while my friend pulled it back out, pointed to the cork, and said, "You didn't put it in far enough." TWSS

A couple of weeks ago, my little brother got a Coney from Sonic. He opened it, took a look at it, and said, "Wow, this is big. I don't know if I can fit this in my mouth." TWSS

As my friend was eating a Popsicle, I hit his hand and he gagged a little. He then said, "If it went any deeper, I probably would have thrown up all over it." TWSS

Last summer, as I was walking out of my church's youth building with another girl, I asked if I could have a sip of her drink. She said, "You can try! I've been sucking on this thing for ten minutes and haven't gotten anything." TWSS

Today, while eating a Greek salad, I said to my friend, "Here, try some." She put it in her mouth and screamed, "It's too salty! I can't swallow it all!" TWSS

A friend of mine made various desserts, and this one girl tried them all and then said, "The white one doesn't taste any different from the black one." TWSS

At a cross-country team party, we were using marshmallow roasters to melt holes in plastic cups. Somebody took a plastic cup with lemonade in it and started to poke a hole in it. When the lemonade started flowing out of the hole, he yelled, "It's starting to spray! Shit, I can't get it out!" TWSS

Yesterday I went to the dentist and today I was having a major toothache on the right side of my mouth. Forgetting about my teeth, I took a bite of a Caesar salad wrap that was too big for my mouth. I was struggling chewing it, and my friend asked me if I was okay. When I was done chewing I responded, "Oh, wow, that was so huge, but I just had to put it all in my mouth." TWSS

My brother was eating a foot-long hotdog and my mom was like, "Wow, that's a big wiener to be putting in your mouth." TWSS

I was at someone's apartment party and there was leftover French bread on the table. It was incredibly stale. My friend was so hungry that she helped herself. After a few minutes of gnawing she turned to me and said, "This is so hard, but I'm so hungry I'd put anything in my mouth." TWSS

Today I was talking to my friend Sidney about her messenger picture. It was of her blowing a bubble with bubble gum. I commented on it and she said, "Yeah, but I've blown bigger ones, just didn't take pictures." TWSS

The other day a friend of mine was drinking a vanilla milk shake. The milk shake was too thick to go through the straw. She was getting annoyed, and said, "I'm sucking but nothing is coming in my mouth!" TWSS

At lunch the other day, my sister ordered a triple-decker sandwich. Once her food arrived she looked at her sandwich and said, "Wow, I'm going to have to prepare myself so I don't choke on all that meat." TWSS

I was eating corn on the cob with my family at dinner. Everyone was using the holders that go in the sides of the corn, except my little sister because she was complaining that they were too hard to put in. My mom said, "Would you stop using your hands and just stick the damn thing in!" TWSS

I was watching the Food Network and the host was making mini doughnuts. After applying the cinnamon-sugar coating, she said, "And now it's ready to pop in my mouth . . . mmm." TWSS

My wife was talking about those thick fruit smoothie drinks and how sometimes the straws get clogged: "You suck and suck and suddenly you get a load in the back of your throat." TWSS

My friend's soda bottle overflowed all
over the table and I started laughing. She
looked up at me in embarrassment and
said, "Well, I tried to get it all in my mouth
before it made a mess, but it came out so
fast." TWSS

Fun and Games

She's Very Active . . .
In More Ways Than One

Today during tennis
practice I heard
the coach help out a
beginner by saying,
"Make sure your grip on
the shaft is tight and
your strokes are long
and hard." TWSS

One of my friends invited me to a lock-in at his church and they had Guitar Hero. Everyone else was getting food and hanging out, but we wanted to go play Guitar Hero before everyone else came back. Apparently my friend's not very good at it, and he didn't know that I am. Since there was only one guitar, we were going to have to take turns, so he said, "Okay, do you want to suck first or should I?" TWSS

My friend and I were playing lacrosse for the first time, and when I finally caught it I said, "God, what a good feeling when it goes in." TWSS

So I was showing my little cousin a football and she grabbed it and said, "It's so big, brown, and hard to grip." TWSS

114

My track friends and I were talking about hurdling. One person said, "I don't think I could get my legs over the top of those hurdles!" Another girl said, "Oh well, I am used to spreading my legs." TWSS

My friend was talking about his hockey game earlier that day. He began to describe a point in the game when he checked another player. He began: "I hit that guy so hard, and then he went down on me." TWSS

I had done a lot of lunges last night, so my legs and butt were hurting really bad. I came to school the next day limping and my friend asked me why I was walking funny. I said, "Man, my butt is so sore from last night that I can't even walk." TWSS

I was at volleyball practice the other day and we were working on rotations. One of the girls was put on the front line and said, "I prefer it in the back." TWSS

That's What She Said

I was at a girls' basketball game, and as I was leaving one of the teams was shooting free throws. I walked in front of the shooting team's bench as the girl missed the shot. Her coach encouraged her by yelling out, "That's okay. Just a little deeper in the hole next time!" TWSS

One of my friends came to my house right after a college basketball game at her school in Long Beach. She had Long Beach painted on her face and wanted to paint it on me, too. Our conversation right before: "Where do you want to put it?" "That's what she said!" "No, but really, I have to know before I get it wet!" TWSS

My friend was trying to get another friend to come to his improv team's game. She asked him if it was his first time playing. He said, "Well, if it will get you to come, sure it's my first time." TWSS

Fun and Games

We were playing soccer in P.E. when this girl fell. The teacher yelled, "Gosh, if you're gonna be on your back the whole time, then don't even bother!" TWSS

Today my friend pitched in a baseball game. When we were back in the dugout he said, "My arm is so tired, it feels like it's about to fall off." TWSS

My friend was playing with a Rubik's Cube, and she said, "Geez, it just keeps getting harder and harder the more you play with it!" TWSS

I was in my karate class, and we were practicing using weapons, which we call our "sticks." Our sensei was explaining a defense against an attack, and said, "Face your partner and simultaneously raise your sticks. Then as your partner jabs at you with his stick, move inside so as to avoid the full impact. Then use your left hand to grab their stick, while simultaneously shoving your stick into your partner's face." TWSS

I was teaching my friend how to play the kazoo. I said, "Put your mouth on this end and instead of just blowing you're gonna hum, then blow. You'll feel it vibrate a little if you're doing it right. But don't get the part in the hole wet because then it won't work no matter how much you blow, and if you blow too hard it comes right out." TWSS

Today I was looking through an app on Facebook called Pieces of Flair, and there was a "piece of flair" for tennis lovers that said, "I love the smell of fresh balls in the morning." TWSS

Today I was playing Scrabble with my friend. She had an X tile and could not find a place to put it. She said, "I could make sex, but it doesn't fit anywhere." TWSS

My friend was trying out for lacrosse. A girl came up to him in class and asked, "Why is your stick shorter than the rest I've seen?" TWSS

Fun and Games

My friend and I were watching a scary movie. I got up to get a drink from the kitchen and he started screaming my name. I ran back into the room and he said, "I kept screaming your name, but you wouldn't come!" TWSS

A few of my friends and I were talking about sports we liked. After five minutes of discussing, one of my friends simply said, "I love anything with balls." TWSS

I ate a lot before jump-roping and threw up a little in my mouth. Afterward I told my friends what had happened, adding, "It's okay, though, I just swallowed it and kept going like a trooper." TWSS

The other day, my bestie and I were playing the Xbox 360 game Spyro. She was playing Spyro and I was playing Cynder. One of Cynder's elements that he uses to kill the enemies is wind, so I yelled, "Oh! Oh my God! I'm blowing all these guys!" TWSS

That's What She Said

I was playing Call of Duty with a friend, and his sister came into the room and asked if I had beat the game already. I said no. She replied, "I could beat it for you if you want me to." TWSS

Today after workouts the school sports trainer was stretching my shoulder. I felt a sharp pain in my shoulder blade, and I asked, "Is it supposed to hurt like that?" He said, "It will only hurt the first couple of times." TWSS

My friend and I were playing sand volleyball, and he was explaining to me the difference in the height of a women's net versus a men's net. My friend said that the men's net gets tied to the top peg on the volleyball post, and I told him that that doesn't seem much higher. My friend replied, "I know it's only a couple of inches, but it makes a big difference." TWSS

My friend and I decided to hook up my old N64. Most of you should know that you have to blow on the game to get it to work. After my friend was blowing on it for a few minutes without it working, we just assumed it was broken. Then she said, "Let's play the PS2, at least with disks when it doesn't work you don't spend twenty minutes blowing just to be screwed." TWSS

While swapping childhood stories with my friend, he remarked how much he used to love riding on the carousel. He said, "Oh, I loved it. I could ride that thing all day long." TWSS

My friends and I went sledding the other day, and after sledding for about thirty minutes I said, "I can't feel my thighs or my ass, but I want to go again!" TWSS

Several of my friends were watching a movie at my dorm. When my roommate went to take the DVD out before the movie was over, one of the girls said, "You can put it in or take it out, but either way you're not going to sleep tonight." TWSS

I was at the park with my friends. They took the swings, so I took the monkey bars and sat on top of them. My friend told me to get off of the bars, and I said no. Later she said, "I'm waiting for you to go down. I don't care how long it takes, I got all day." TWSS

I had just finished my cross-country race and was eating a cookie. I had to run a cool down with three other girls but had already started eating the cookie. I started running and said, "Oh my God, slow down, this is just too hard. You don't understand, it's really hard and I keep missing my mouth! It just won't go in while I'm moving!" TWSS

My friend and I were in gym class. We were playing basketball and someone slung the ball right at my face. I dove and hit the floor. The ball hit my friend in the face. He yelled, "Ow! Why am I always the one taking balls to the face?!" TWSS

A few of my friends and I were at the movies, and one friend ordered a large nachos. The guy brought it out and she said, "It's too big, I don't think I can handle it." TWSS

My son was learning to snowboard and falling frequently. When we were on the chairlift late in the day I asked him how he was enjoying it. He said, "My ass is really sore, but I like it a lot." TWSS

I was playing a drinking game with my friends. In the course of play, one of the girls needed to finish her drink, and since she still had a full can, we decided to try to make her chug the whole thing. Halfway through she stopped and said, "I can't keep it in my mouth." TWSS

On an old newspaper ad for a joystick game, the title said, "The longer you play with it, the harder it gets." TWSS

A few years back my uncle and cousins took us out to play mini golf. My sister was doing a really good job and my uncle said to my dad, "Wow, she's really good at working those balls! She's going to be a pro when she gets older." TWSS

A friend was getting ready to tell a story about an amazing racquetball shot. He started out by giving a brief description of the game for those unfamiliar with it. When describing the court he said, "It's twice as long as it is wide." TWSS

Today I was teaching a couple of my friends how to make origami tulips. When we got to the last step—inflating the tulip—my friends had no trouble, but since mine was smaller, it was more difficult. They were laughing at me, to which I responded, "Yeah, well, they're easier to blow when they're big." TWSS

A few friends and I were playing golf. We were headed to the next hole and my friend said, "I've never done this hole before." TWSS

Fun and Games

I saw my favorite band, The Morning Of, today. The stage was higher than normal and the singer kept singing on his knees. He said, "It's so much easier to get to you when I'm on my knees." TWSS

I was playing with my lacrosse team and my friend spat out her mouth guard, saying, "This thing is too big and hard and it makes me gag!" TWSS

My rowing coach constantly gets mad at us for slouching in the boat, which causes problems. All throughout practice we can hear him shouting, "You need to be long and hard or else it won't go in right and you won't be able to pull out right!" TWSS

My roommate and I were playing an intense game of Halo 3 on Boundary. We were both underground, and he was posted up underneath the tunnel in the middle with a shotgun waiting for the other team to jump in, when he yelled, "Go ahead, come in my hole!" TWSS

My friend had just gotten one of those ping-pong tables where you can fold half of it up and practice. He then told me in a chat, "I'm gonna go to the basement now and play with myself." TWSS

The other day I was at my cousin's birthday party. My brother and I were blowing up balloons. My sister came in and said, "No one blows better than me!" TWSS

I was at my friend's playing Super Nintendo when the game stopped working. She took it out and started blowing air into the game slot. When it still wouldn't work she yelled, "God, how many times do I have to blow this thing to make it turn on!?" TWSS

While playing Call of Duty my friend said, "I can't go two minutes without getting railed from behind." TWSS

My friend and I were playing mini golf. After I missed a shot, my friend yelled out, "Wow, two holes and you miss them both." TWSS

At the rock-climbing wall, somebody had moved the fake plastic climbing rocks around in a new way. He was showing another person how he had arranged them and said, "It's great because there's a ton of positions and it's still really satisfying." TWSS

That's What *He* Said

Sometimes He's Doing All the Talking

Today we were learning probability in my math class. Discussing the probability of flipping a coin, my teacher said, "What are my chances of getting head three times?" TWHS

Today our band director was yelling at us and said, "From up here it sounds like you're sucking. Start blowing." TWHS

Today I was driving in my car with my mom. I was drinking a Slushee and started coughing, so I spit it back out. My mom said, "Why don't you try swallowing for once? I hate when you spit it out because it gets everywhere." TWHS

I was channel surfing and caught a man simulating a murder using a gardening tool and testing how strong its impact would be. He said, "I got some significant blows with that hoe." TWHS

At a dance we recently had, my friend invited a girl he thought was cute to go with him, but she told him she didn't want to go at all and seemed kind of embarrassed about it. In the car he turned to me and said, "I don't know why she wouldn't come, I'm not *that* bad." TWHS

My friend and I were plugging a flash drive into the back of a Mac computer. She said, "I hate putting it in the back because I can't see where the hole is." TWHS

I was at lunch and one of my coworkers stated, "You know, you can't fit an entire orange in your mouth." After pausing, he added, "You think your mouth's big enough, but it's not." TWHS

The other day in my sculpture class, my friend was getting ready to paint his plaster sculpture. He wasn't sure if there was a certain way to paint it, so he asked, "Do you have to get it wet first or can you just go at it?" TWHS

My sister was trying to unclog the toilet with a plunger. She hadn't used one before, so my mom was trying to help her. My mom asked her if she already knew how to do it, and she replied, "All I know is that I should stick it in as far as I can, and fast, too." TWHS

Once after a long workout for track, my friend complained, "My thighs are sooo freaking sore." (TWSS) My other friend standing next to us replied, "It's okay. It's your first time, it'll get better." TWHS

Today I was at the dentist, and while he was filling a cavity he said, "I bet it's hard to swallow while I'm still in your mouth." TWHS

My friend was telling me how if she were a cookie she'd eat herself. My other friend walked up, having missed her statement, but just in time to hear me say, "Well, if you tasted good enough, I'd eat you all the time." TWHS

I was surprised to see my wife on the elliptical machine, and she said, "Don't worry, this won't last long, I haven't done this in a while." TWHS

Today I was at the dentist getting my teeth cleaned. When my dentist was ready he said, "Open wide so I can stick it in there good." TWHS

A few weeks ago at school, there was an assembly addressing several issues. All of the students were sitting on the gym floor, and after a while we started to get annoyed. The principal noticed this and said, "Be patient. I know it's hard and the floor is uncomfortable, but I'm almost finished." TWHS

I was at Applebee's and my sister ordered a steak medium-rare, saying, "I like it when it's pink and juicy." My mom said to her, "I didn't think you were the pink and juicy type of person." My sister replied, "It has to be pink and juicy or I won't enjoy it." TWHS

133

At lunch one day at school I was eating a vanilla yogurt. As I was eating, my friend next to me said, "Wow, you sucked that down fast." TWHS

My bestie and I were watching a jeans ad, and there was a man wearing skinny jeans. I commented, "Ooh, that's a tight fit." TWHS

At practice all of my teammates usually huddle around the fan at break. One day my friends and I decided to give the fan a name as a joke. Later that day someone came over to the fan and didn't use the name, so we told her what it was. She then responded with, "I don't care what the name is. I just want it to blow me." TWHS

My friends and I were sitting in math class and one of my friends was acting as though she understood what we were doing. My other friend turned to her and said, "You're really bad at faking things!" TWHS

Today in my health class we had to go the whole class breathing through straws to demonstrate lung problems caused by smoking. This one obnoxious kid kept taking his straw out and talking. The teacher said, "We need to do this quietly. Now put it back in your mouth and don't take it out until we're finished!" TWHS

I'm from England and now live in America. You know how the British call erasers "rubbers"? Well, in the middle of a dead silent test, I asked, "Does anyone have a rubber I can borrow? I will give it back after I'm finished with it." TWHS

My neighbor was working on a brake line under his car. He asked me for a wire brush to scrape off the rust before repairing it. After fixing the line, he came out from under the car and said, "I'm a little rusty, I'm surprised it didn't blow sooner." TWHS

My friend Sarah was having a very difficult time during her math test. Eventually, she couldn't stand the fact that this one question was too hard for her. So she marched straight up to the teacher and said, "Mr. Meyer, it's just too hard and I can't bear it any longer. Can you just remove it?" (TWSS) To which he replied, "I'm sorry. You'll just have to bear with it. I know it's hard, but it's just as hard for everybody else." TWHS

The lunch bell rang, and my friend still had half of her fries. She said, "I don't have time to finish this," and my other friend replied, "Just shove it all in your mouth and swallow." TWHS

My brother was stacking Lego men's heads up onto a stick. He happily announced, "Look how much head I got!" TWHS

Today at school, after a very unproductive class, my teacher loudly and angrily pointed out, "Well, I didn't get as far as I wanted, but that rarely happens anyway." TWHS

136

The other day I was getting my first tattoo, and I was really tense and scared. At first it was difficult for me to stop being tense, so I said, "I'll be tense at first, then I'll loosen up." (TWSS) The tattoo artist replied, "It's okay, I can pull out fast." TWHS

A few days ago in P.E., we were in the weight room and there were some giant exercise balls. I ran to get the biggest ball and my friend said, "I know you like balls, but be gentle." TWHS

My buddy and I were in class one day and he had a Hershey's Kiss in his hand. I tried to knock it out but he moved his hand and ate the chocolate. After this failed attempt, I said, "I tried to pop it up before you put it in your mouth." TWHS

My best friend was telling us how she almost choked on a carrot, and my friend Nick said, "So I guess you can't be trusted with anything bigger in your mouth." TWHS

I was eating a sub sandwich at my grandma's house. As I took a bite, some lettuce fell out, and she said, "Don't tell me you can't fit it all in, your mouth is big enough!" TWHS

Today I was doing an arts and crafts thing with my friends, but when I tried to get some glue, it wouldn't come out of the bottle. My friend told me, "Just rub it to get it warm. But be careful, we don't want white stuff everywhere." TWHS

While driving, my grandmother noticed a sign for eight-dollar hand washes at a car wash. She said, "Wow, eight dollars is cheap for a hand job!" TWHS

So the other day my dad and I were putting hamburger in Ziploc bags to freeze for later. He turned to me and said, "Here, just hold it open while I slide the meat in." TWHS

Today in school my gym class played volleyball. At the end of the period, we were in the locker room and my friend told me, "Great job. You were really pounding those balls out there." TWHS

I was at work where there is not much room to move around in the back room. This girl said, "Nick, can you get out before I get in?" TWHS

Last winter my friends and I were walking down the street and we saw a small tunnel built out of snow. My friends dared me to go in and I said, "No way! I'm not even going to try to go in there because I know I'm too big and I'll get stuck and I won't be able to get out. Then what would we do?" TWHS

My friend was borrowing my boyfriend's bike and kept complaining about how small it was. My boyfriend got annoyed and said, "If it's so small, then why are you riding it?!" TWHS

My mom was painting my new shed this afternoon and she said, "My hand and arm are getting tired." (TWSS) My dad said, "We're almost done, keep stroking." TWHS

My older cousin came to visit and we were driving in the car talking about how my brother couldn't roll his "r"s. We tried to teach him how to roll his "r"s and had little success. My cousin said, "If you can't do it with your tongue, do it with your throat." TWHS

My boyfriend and I were getting ready to go out, but I was having trouble getting my earring backing on, as I have two holes in each ear. Frustrated, I exclaimed, "This is so confusing when there are two holes!" TWHS

The other day I was at a shoe store with my friend. I was trying on heels that had a tiny buckle on them, and I was having a hard time with it. I said, "I see the hole, but I can't get it in!" TWHS

The other day I was playing NBA 2K9 on Xbox Live. The person I was playing against picked the Lakers and decided to drive to the basket for a layup. When he went too far under the hoop and hit the ball on the bottom of the rim, he said, "Damn, I penetrated too far!" TWHS

I was standing near some friends, and one was giving the other a spontaneous back massage. The girl getting the massage asked the other girl to press harder. The masseuse, whose fingers were getting tired, said, "I won't be able to last long if I keep pushing this hard." TWHS

My sister and I were doing the dishes and she was trying to pull a pan out of the dishwasher. She was struggling and making a lot of noise, so my dad came over to see what she was doing. When he saw her trying to get the pan out of the dishwasher he said, "Stop jerking it so hard. It's gonna break!" TWHS

Today my friend and I were eating sour grapes. I didn't want to eat any, and I told my friend. She said, "It's not that big. Stick it in your mouth and suck it 'til the juice comes out." TWHS

Two of my friends and I were going through the checkout stand at our local grocery store, and the cashier asked me to put the change in the donation box. The change didn't go in and I said, "I put it in the hole, but it came back out." TWHS

My teacher invited a guest speaker to class last week, but no one showed up. Today he vented his frustrations to us and told us that the speaker will come back next week. He firmly said, "Do you have any idea how long and hard I had to work to get her to come? Let alone twice!" TWHS

I had all my books in my backpack and could barely fit it in my locker. After finally getting it in my locker my friend told me that we leave our stuff in our homeroom. I replied, "I worked that hard getting it in, I'm not taking it out." TWHS

I play softball on a couple of coed teams. One game I was needed as the catcher, which I've never played before. I got hit in the face, then again, and again. By the end of the double header, I had taken a beating. In the dugout my husband said, "Wow, baby, you sure were a trooper taking all those balls to the face." TWHS

In Popular Culture

She's So Hot Right Now

I was listening to the new song "Ego" by Beyoncé. In the song she sings, "It's too big, it's too wide, it's too strong, it won't fit, it's too much, it's too tough." TWSS

My friends and I went to see the new Harry Potter movie and Dumbledore said, "Just no matter what, keep making me take it. Even if you have to shove it down my throat." TWSS

I was watching *MythBusters,* and they were trying to make a crossbow out of newspaper, underwear elastic, and a plastic food tray. Then they were going to shoot it into ballistics gel. Adam said, "I would be happy with two inches of penetration." (TWSS) Then Jamie said, "I wouldn't." TWSS

Today Tyler Florence on Food Network said, "It's easier to use your hand . . . it's faster." TWSS

One day I was at home watching *iCarly*. Spencer said, "I'm gonna go take a shower." Freddie asked why, and Spencer said, "I do my best thinking when I'm wet." TWSS

Today some friends and I were watching the movie *Fools Rush In*. Matthew Perry's character is thrown up on by a baby. As he's cleaning himself up, he says, "I didn't know so much could come out of something that small." TWSS

I was watching *Toy Story* and Sid (the bad next-door neighbor kid) was talking about receiving his rocket in the mail. He exclaimed, "It came, it finally came . . . THE BIG ONE." TWSS

I was watching *Star Wars: A New Hope* on TV, and in it Obi Wan says, "This little one's not worth the effort." TWSS

In an episode of *The Office*, Michael and Jan are sitting together with a bunch of other Dunder Mifflin employees at a paper convention. Jan: "I can't stay on top of you 24/7." TWSS

Today we were watching *The Magic School Bus* in biology while talking about chloroplasts. When the chloroplast popped, the girl said, "It's all white and sticky! It got in my mouth, I liked it!" TWSS

We were watching the movie *The Alamo,* and when Davy Crockett is captured and about to be killed, he says, "I want to warn you all, I'm a screamer." TWSS

Today, while watching *The Little Mermaid*, I just noticed the line in the song "Under the Sea" where Sebastian sings, "Darling it's better down where it's wetter, take it from me." TWSS

In Popular Culture

In *Gladiator*, Commodus says, "I've searched the faces of the gods for ways to please you." TWSS

I was watching *Malcolm in the Middle*. In one scene Dewey answers the phone and says, "It's been in your mouth for half an hour! Either spit it out or swallow it!" TWSS

I was listening to the song "Hot N Cold" by Katy Perry. Some of the lyrics are: "You're in, then you're out. You're up, then you're down." TWSS

The other day while watching the movie *Cars* for the hundredth time with my sisters, I noticed the line "Put it in deep and don't pull out." TWSS

Today I was watching Rachael Ray. She said, "I can't wait to slide that warm thing into my mouth." TWSS

I was watching NBC right after the U.S. Open and a commentator said this about Tiger's performance: "Too bad Tiger forgot how to properly stroke, I guess he's not as good as he was before." TWSS

I was watching a KFC ad about the new "sandwich" with two pieces of chicken around bacon and cheese. The fellow said, "It takes two to fill me up!" TWSS

Today in the newspaper comics there was a *Get Fuzzy* cartoon where the dog wanted to eat something that the cat had. The cat kept telling him it wasn't edible, while the dog kept saying that he didn't care because dogs will eat just about anything. Finally the cat insists it was never edible, and after a pause the dog says, "Who am I kidding, if it fits in my mouth I'll give it a go." TWSS

Watching *American Idol*. Casey James is singing, "Hold On, I'm Coming." TWSS

In Popular Culture

I was watching *That '70s Show* and Red
was stoned out of his mind. At one point he
sprayed a fire extinguisher and he smiled
really proudly and exclaimed, "Wow, that
really shot out of there!" TWSS

Last night I was watching *Twilight Saga: New
Moon*. In the scene where Edward breaks up with
Bella, he mentions leaving and not taking her with
him. Bella protests, saying "I'm coming!" (TWHS)
To which Edward says, "No, I don't want you to
come!" TWSS

I was watching *SuperNanny,* and in the show the nanny
told the father that his way of getting his son's attention
was wrong. While gesturing pulling his arm she said,
"You jerk him 'til he comes." TWSS

When Luke and the Rebel fighters are
attacking the Death Star in *Star Wars:
Episode IV*, one of the fighter pilots says
to Luke, "At that speed, will you be able to
pull out in time?" TWSS

I was watching *10 Things I Hate About You*, and the episode was about a school dance. Originally, the girl did not want to go to the dance, but her date convinced her to go. During the slow-dance scene, she sweetly tilts her head up at him and says, "I'm so glad you made me come." TWSS

I was watching *Family Guy* and Lois had been thrown in jail for shoplifting. When explaining herself later in the prison, she says, "I felt like I had a void in my life, like there was a secret hole in me. And I was trying to fill that hole with all kinds of expensive objects and things. And I felt wonderful with all those things filling that hole." TWSS

Today I was trying to find the *Twilight Eclipse* trailer, and I found a video for the film *Whip It*. It was titled: "Whip It Out Soon." TWSS

Today I realized *America's Next Top Model*'s theme song says, "You wanna be on top?" TWSS

Lifehouse's lyrics to "Whatever It Takes" are: "If we're gonna make this work, you've got to let me inside, even though it hurts." TWSS

I was watching deleted scenes from *The Office* on DVD. In one episode, Dwight is talking to the camera about how hard it is for him to make sure Michael has a good birthday every year: "He gets very excited, but he's also under a lot of pressure, which builds up until he's ready to explode . . . it's my job to release that pressure, so he can enjoy himself, if only for a moment." TWSS

Throughout History

Famous Quotes from Dirty Minds

"The time for action has arrived, stop thinking and go in."

—Napoleon Bonaparte, French emperor (1769-1821)

"Well, I ride just a couple times a week."
— Evel Knievel, daredevil (1938–2007)

"His body was elastic and he could make his extremities as long as he wanted. As a youngster I didn't fully appreciate [it]."
— Ben Affleck, actor (1972–present)

"This will gratify some people and astonish the rest."
— Mark Twain, author (1835–1910)

"'Oh my God, that's huge! It's bigger than huge.' I was kind of freaked out at first."
— Kristen Stewart, actress (1990–present)

"You've got to push yourself harder . . . You've got to take the tools you have and probe deeper."
— William Albert Allard, world-renowned photographer (1937–present)

"He hath eaten me out."
— William Shakespeare (from *Henry IV*, Part 2), playwright (1564–1616)

"When you are as great as I am it is hard to be humble."
— Muhammad Ali, world-champion boxer (1942–present)

"I want to top expectations. I want to blow you away."
— Quentin Tarantino, director and screenwriter (1963–present)

"Go deeper and even stronger into my treasure mine."
— Zane Grey, author (1872–1939)

That's What She Said

"It's so much fun to perform that you want to do it again and the more you get out of it the better."

—Leo Kottke, musician (1945–present)

"I know I'm going to blow one day."
—Mike Tyson, world-champion boxer (1966–present)

"Go through the hole."
—John F. Kennedy, 35th president of the United States (1917–1963)

"Be more splendid, more extraordinary. Use every moment to fill yourself up."
—Oprah Winfrey, TV host, actress, and philanthropist (1954–present)

"Get thee behind me."

—Bible, Matthew 16:23

"I want the cream to rise."

—Robert Frost, poet (1874–1963)

"I would love to have the ability to make you sore."

—Tiger Woods, golfer (1975–present)

"I don't mind gays. But I don't want 'em stuffing it down my throat all the time."
　　—Chris Buttars, Utah state senator (1942–present)

"Wow, I cannot believe it. This is much bigger than I thought it would be. You know what I'm going to do tonight. . . I'm going to go home, and I'm going to find a special place to put this. I'll be completely honest with you, I wanted this so bad I could taste it. Thank you, this is a true honor and I'm glad I came."
　　　　　　　　　　—Steve Carell, actor (1962–present)

"I'm sure I'm not as good or as experienced as other actresses, but everybody has to start somewhere."
　　　　　　　—Claudia Schiffer, supermodel (1970–present)

"I may be drunk . . . but in the morning I will be sober and you will still be ugly."
　　　　　　—Winston Churchill, British prime minister
　　　　　　　　　　　　　　　　　　(1874–1965)

"Imma let you finish."
　　　　　　　　—Kanye West, rapper (1977–present)

That's What She Said

"And then I thrust in my head. Oh, you would have laughed to see how cunningly I thrust it in!"
— Edgar Allan Poe (from "The Tell-Tale Heart"),
writer (1809–1849)

Appendix 1

Add Your Own!

Personalize your copy of *That's What She Said* by adding in your very own "that's what she said" stories!

Your story: _____

_____

_____

_____

_____

_____

_____

_____. TWSS

Appendix 1

Your story: _____

_____

_____

_____

_____

_____

_____. TWSS

Your story: _____

_____

_____

_____

_____

_____

_____. TWSS

Appendix 1

Your story: _____

_____

_____

_____

_____

_____

_____

_____. TWSS

Your story: _____

_____

_____

_____

_____

_____

_____

_____. TWSS

Appendix 1

Your story: _____

_____

_____

_____

_____

_____

_____. TWSS

Your story: _____

_____

_____

_____

_____

_____

_____. TWSS

Appendix 1

Your story: _____

_____

_____

_____

_____

_____

_____

_____. TWSS

Your story: _____

_____

_____

_____

_____

_____

_____. TWSS

Appendix 1

Your story: _____

_____

_____

_____

_____

_____

_____

_____. TWSS

Your story: _____

_____

_____

_____

_____

_____

_____

_____. TWSS

Appendix 1

Your story: _____

_____

_____

_____

_____

_____

_____

_____. TWSS

Your story: _____

_____

_____

_____

_____

_____

_____

_____. TWSS

Appendix 1

Your story: _____

_____

_____

_____

_____

_____

_____

_____. TWSS

Your story: _____

_____

_____

_____

_____

_____

_____

_____. TWSS

Appendix 1

Your story: _____

_____

_____

_____

_____

_____

_____

_____. TWSS

Your story: _____

_____

_____

_____

_____

_____

_____

_____. TWSS

Appendix 1

Your story: _____

_____

_____

_____

_____

_____

_____

_____. TWSS

Your story: _____

_____

_____

_____

_____

_____

_____

_____. TWSS

Appendix 2

The That's What She Said Personality Quiz

Do you want to know what type of that's what she said joke most closely matches your personality and inner desires? Take the following quiz to discover your TWSS joke soul mate.

1. *What is your idea of the perfect first date?*

   ____a. A juicy steak dinner, the more meat the better

   ____b. A long walk on the beach, your feet won't be the only thing that gets wet

   ____c. A round of miniature golf, because you like watching balls go into holes

   ____d. Ballroom dancing

2. *What did you want to be when you grew up?*

   ____a. A professional athlete, muscular and thick-headed

_____b. An Olympic swimmer, able to finish in sixty seconds flat

_____c. A surgeon, specializing in removing and reinserting certain organs

_____d. An elementary school teacher

3. If you could be an animal, which one would you be?

_____a. A lion, ruler of the beasts and always on the prowl

_____b. A dolphin, frolicking in the water

_____c. A prairie dog, cautiously poking your head in and out of holes all day long

_____d. A puppy

4. Imagine you are a high school swim coach. Which of the following are you most likely to say to your team to pump them up before a big meet?

_____a. "It may look long to you now, but it'll be over before you know it."

_____b. "Make sure you get a little wet first before you start. It'll be more comfortable for you that way."

_____c. "Make sure you have a clean entry, and

keep up a powerful stroking motion until you finish."

____d. "Even if you lose today, you're all still winners in my book."

5. *If you could have one superpower, what would it be?*

____a. Extreme flexibility, able to transform and stretch any part of your body at will

____b. Ability to breathe underwater, so you never need to come up for air

____c. Invisibility, so you can get in and out of tight places without detection

____d. I'm happy just the way I am.

6. *What is your favorite food?*

____a. A foot-long hot dog, because the regular-size ones just won't do

____b. A juicy watermelon, as long as it doesn't get all over my face

____c. I'll eat practically anything, so long as it fits in my mouth

____d. A salad

7. What quality do you find most attractive in a romantic partner?

_____a. A sexy body, enough said

_____b. Their mouth, it's luscious, moist, and capable of so many things

_____c. A charming personality, because it's what's on the inside that counts

_____d. A good sense of humor

Now count up the number of A's, B's, C's, and D's you checked above and match the highest total to your TWSS joke personality type below!

Total A's: _____
Total B's: _____
Total C's: _____
Total D's: _____

Your That's What She Said Personality Type

Big Man or Woman on Campus (*Mostly A's*): You are only satisfied with the very best and have a rather large . . . ego, among other things. You find yourself laughing the hardest at TWSS jokes that are laced with innuendo about the size of everyday objects.

The Wetter the Better (*Mostly B's*): On a hot summer day, you can often be found soaking up some rays on the beach or cooling off in whatever body of water you can find. Your TWSS joke of choice reflects your passion for getting wet.

In & Out (*Mostly C's*): You know how to have fun and are the life of the party, because you have a knack for effortlessly slipping TWSS jokes in and out of practically every conversation you're a part of.

Sweet & Innocent (*Mostly D's*): You are honest and loyal and you often wear your heart on your sleeve. When it comes to TWSS jokes, you are slightly gullible, and it might take you longer than most to catch on to the double meaning.